30 Days to Property Success

by Paul Baldry with Andrew McInnes

For
Eva-Mae, William, Lilia, Harriet
and Frayer

Who attested that I was an author
long before it became reality.

First published by Property Success Ltd
This edition published 2018 by Property Success Ltd
Laburnum Terrace
Ashington
NE63 0XX

ISBN 978-1-9999828-0-5

Printed in Peterborough, England

Biographies

Paul Baldry is someone whose life goal was to retire while young enough to enjoy it. Property was the way to achieve this and he retired at the age of just 29! Since then he has found the time to open various branches of his estate agency, while buying further properties. He also enjoys training and mentoring others through their property journey and financial success. Paul lives in Northumberland, but enjoys travelling throughout the UK, Europe, Asia and America.

Andrew McInnes is an author, property investor, journalist and public speaker. He bought his first investment property in 2001 and has built up a sizeable portfolio of properties in the UK and overseas. He has been a regular contributor to property magazines over the past decade and co-authored the Amazon No.1 best-seller The Serviced Accommodation Success Manual with Paul Smith in the summer of 2017. He has hosted numerous property networking events and divides his time between property training, writing and running his various businesses. He lives in Troon, South Ayrshire, Scotland.

Foreword by Andy McInnes:

If you asked me for one good reason, in one word, to learn how to invest in property it would be 'freedom'. That is, freedom from the daily grind; freedom from worrying about paying all the bills; freedom from that wave of panic that hits you on a Sunday evening when you realise you'll be back to a job you hate the following morning, supervised by a boss you have absolutely no respect for and working with people with whom you have very little in common.

You can choose to live like that for the rest of your working days (if your occupation even has a long-term future) or you can take your destiny in your own hands and follow our step-by-step process to setting up a fully systemised property business that you will be in total control of. Your future self will thank you very much. We promise.

You owe it to yourself to design your own life, rather than letting someone else create it for you. Very few of us knew about investing when we were going through the education system, and that's because that system was and is designed to place you in a convenient box marked 'employee', whether you like it or not.

But you have no excuses now for just following the herd and sticking with a job - any job - as this book will change your life and make you wonder why you never took control of your own destiny earlier. There is a saying, and I paraphrase, that the best time to invest in property was 20/30/40/100 years ago and the second-best time is right now.

Please do not delay your property journey any longer. Time is the most precious commodity that any of us have and procrastination will ensure you'll be sitting down at this time next year and wondering why you just didn't go for it. We've all been there so don't fall into that trap again.

You are reading this book in real time RIGHT NOW, so start acting on the precious knowledge that is entering your subconscious mind. This kind of education is totally pointless unless you put it into practice and that means taking the action steps detailed throughout this book.

We know there are other property books on the market and by all means read them all – after you've finished this one! But with Thirty Days to Property Success we made a conscious decision to get straight to the point with every chapter rather than providing page after page of extraneous facts and figures that only serve to confuse the reader, especially if you are completely new to the wonderful and lucrative world of property.

Rather than provide you with screeds of amusing anecdotes (we'll save those for when you meet us in person) we have provided a step-by-step guide to getting you on the property ladder as quickly as possible. Unlike other property books, we don't arrogantly assume that you are interested in our life stories and how nice we are to animals and small children. Again, when you come on our course or discovery events, we'll be happy to chew the fat about anything you like over a coffee (Paul) or a beer (Andy).

Instead of padding this book out with 'filler' material that would only serve to insult your considerable intelligence, we focused on brevity and simplicity, although not at the expense of clarity. I have a professional background in writing and editing for tabloid newspapers where space is at a premium and every single word must pull its weight. So, we can guarantee that everything you'll need to set up a sustainable property business within 30 days is contained within this book.

In order to provide some fuel for your journey, we have designed most of the chapters to be interactive, so you can take action right away on every step of your journey. The authors also pledge to respond quickly to any and all queries within 48 hours. We believe we've already provided the answers for any queries you may have but the property business can change very quickly, and depending on what edition of the book you are reading, some of the legislation referred to may have become obsolete. We will provide links to the latest rules and regulations in your area of operations, so don't be too concerned about this.

Thirty Days to Property Success has been designed to be read in linear fashion (i.e. start with Chapter One and don't be tempted to skip any sections). We couldn't be clearer about this as our methodology of property investment is time-tested and the instructions should be strictly followed as presented. We're not a Quentin Tarantino film where the timelines are all over the place, so please follow the action steps as detailed or else you may risk getting gunned down in a warehouse by career criminals wearing dark suits and black ties.

Don't forget that we're in your corner and we want you to succeed as a property investor. We all started out as amateurs and newbies and, in some way, it's the most exciting part of your quest as you still have it all in front of you. Don't lose sight of the fact that anticipation is a very important part of anyone's life. Of course, your work, your family and your friends are important, but without that tingle of excitement, your existence will lack something – the sauce, the sizzle, the big pay-off. You will be cheating yourself if you refuse to enjoy what's coming; in this case a successful, systemised and future-proof property business that will free up your time to do what you really want to do and earn you the (sometimes grudging) respect of your peers. All that's left to be said in this introduction is to tell you to enjoy the ride.

A little more about Paul Baldry

My earliest memories of money come from the infamous UK Miners Strike of 1984/85, which has been described as the most bitter and violent industrial dispute in British history.

I grew up in a small town in the north east of England called Ashington, where my parents still live. The place had a very strong connection with the coalmining industry and there is a book available about it called: 'Ashington: the world's biggest pit village'.

That Christmas of 1984, right in the middle of the strike the union for miners (the NUM or National Union of Mineworkers) gave out presents for the miner's families because there was a lot of hardship in the area at the time. The donations came from local people, and some were bought from union funds. As my father later recalled, the friends of the union got their presents first, and what remained was for the rest.

My particular present was two uninflated leather footballs. The problem was that I didn't even like football (and I started to dislike it even more after that). In a practical sense, we didn't own a pump, so I couldn't even blow the footballs up. So by the following June, those uninflated footballs were still lying about in my room, unloved and unused.

That image has always remained in my memory and it's probably the reason I still have no time for football, even after all these years. The enduring memory for me of that time is a sense of the powerlessness that a young child going through such an experience can appreciate.

My time at school was uneventful and anti-climax of academic results and I had various jobs, sales, as I knew I needed to improve my total shyness. Call centre jobs, as it was the jobs available in the area and then I got the opportunity to install computer networks eventually going to London. I worked in various schools, universities and even got to work at Cisco and even the War Cabinet.

Eventually I got a job in a hospital in Newcastle, my time in the NHS was a strange period of my working life in that I was either incredibly busy or I had nothing to do at all. There was never an in-between state of steady work and to be honest, the days were mostly empty in terms of graft and any kind of work satisfaction.

I would sometimes work a day shift, from 8am until 4pm, and I used a computer to print out all of my jobs. Every task had an allotted time period in which you had to complete it, and on plenty of occasions I would have finished every one of my jobs by 10 or 11am. When that happened, I go to see the supervisors and ask if there were any jobs.

In most cases, there were no more tasks to complete and they would say to me: "Go and walk around the hospital and see if there is anything else to do. Lunch is 12 o'clock...' They basically just wanted me out of the way because they had nothing for me to do and, as you can imagine, it was a very unfulfilling way to spend my time.

One guy who I worked alongside during this time could sleep sitting up, and everyone always knew where he was – in a disabled toilet in the far end of the hospital!

So he could hide in there and when he was ever needed, someone was dispatched to 'knock on his office door' as it were. The funny thing is, his leaving do was held at a local pub and after a number of pints, he went to the toilet and fell asleep. The staff hadn't checked the toilets properly and the chap had to climb out a window at 3am the following morning! To me, that always seemed like a fitting conclusion to his job.

Luckily, I worked shifts which occasionally had its advantages. Firstly, it meant I didn't have to play hide-and-seek around the hospital.

Second, it was a small team, which meant if one member was off, another member would cover their shift, so lots of opportunities for overtime - especially as one colleague clearly thought the six months paid sickness was a key part of his employment terms Cortisol was his friend - whether he needed it or not.

And, third, the shift patterns meant I wasn't stuck at work during the day, for viewings, estate agents and showing investors around my local area. The meeting with investors came later in my time at the hospital but proved to be exceptionally important for what I was about to embark on.

My time at the hospital give me a lot of spare mental capacity, although I worked 40, 50, 70 up to hours per week (that's a 16-hour shift Monday through to Saturday and an easy 12 hour shift on Sunday*). I knew people there who had been doing virtually the same thing for 20-30 years, but it just didn't fulfil me.

I just couldn't see myself staying there that long, and some of my shift colleagues advised me to leave too (in the nicest sense). They said to me: "Don't get stuck here like I have, because you are destined for something, at least something better than here."

They also advised me that after you've completed your first five years of service, you are more than likely stuck in the hospital for life. They had seen this happening to so many people, including themselves. I knew I had to get out and I knew I had to find something. But what?

I had been saving my money from the hospital salary and I thought to myself that, whatever happens I need a house and I'm better off buying, rather than renting.

So I went out and purchased a three-bedroom semi-detached property in Widdrington. It was more or less a new-build (only a few years old) and I thought it was the sensible thing to do, especially as I was back living at home with my parents at this time. I needed my space and I thought about a few businesses that would require some space to get off the ground.

I bought this particular property in January 2007 and I then proceeded to spend a fair bit of time to do it up and make it ready to live in, with the assistance of my father. At this point, I was still working stupid hours at the hospital, before driving straight from work to the property and working until 10 or 11 at night.

One day I went to my new property and my father had taken the front and back doors off to plane and paint, and was waiting for them to dry before putting them back up. We were both painting the spindles on the stairs, with a freezing cold wind blowing through the house, when it started to snow!

The wind now brought minus 5-degree Celsius hailstones with a 10-mile an hour wind through the front door and out the back door and straight through me. We had to finish the painting so we kept going past the point where I couldn't even feel my hands. In the end, I had to get my father the open my fingers off the paint brush as they wouldn't move. So I spent five minutes in my car to warm them up and then went back out to re-attach the doors before going home, sleeping, working and then returning to the house. That was certainly a memorable day.

However, one good thing did come from the project that would point me towards my future direction. While we were working on my house, the property next door was sold for £20,000 more than what I had paid – and this was less than a week after I had completion.

My father and I thought this was great news and thought of how we could do this again. It became quite clear very early on that we didn't want to be doing so much work to every property we bought, so we looked at buying and renting as a way to own property and then make money.

Later that day, we broke the news to my mother that I wasn't in fact going to move out but my father and I were going to buy property instead. At a family birthday meal, we made the decision that we would buy a property, see how we got on and then maybe build up to 10 or so, maybe one day get to 20 (10 seemed like such a high number and 20 properties represented a portfolio potentially worth more than £1million).

We were unsure of where to buy so put adverts in newsagents and corner shops saying "One, two and three-bedroom properties available locally. * Gas central heating * Double glazed * DSS accepted * Available now. Call Paul on ………"

We didn't have a property, but we put these ads into every shop in Ashington, Lynemouth, to the North, Newbiggin-by-Sea to the East and Blyth to the South. I ended up having to switch my phone off as I had so many calls and then I had to go back round and take all the adverts down as the demand was so overwhelming!

I had also been going to visit all of the local estate agents and seeing loads of properties. My rationale at the time was that if it's under £80k then I need to see it.

At this early stage, I didn't know what I was going to buy. What town was best? What number of bedrooms was best? Should I buy run down and then do up? Flats v Houses? It was all up in the air so I viewed everything so I could compare and contrast what was out there.

Through just one of those local agents, in the space of 12 months, I had more than 1000 appointments, which averages out at 2.7 viewings, 7 days per week, every week, including Christmas. And when you added in the other five agents I also went on viewings with, I was easily looking at between 40-50 properties per week during my first year (all while working at the hospital).

The upshot was that I put in cheeky offers and waited for what came back. In the end, the first phone call I received led to me buying two properties. In fact, in my first week I agreed four purchases.

We (my father and I) bought 10 properties in a matter of months as everything we read and my excel calculation said there was security in having more properties. You should always aim to spread the risk.

It was a slight difference from what we thought we would do initially, and we learned so much from actually going out there and doing it. On-the-job education really wasn't the best way, there just wasn't any training available at the time. I so wish there was, we wouldn't have made some of the mistakes we made early on.

In our first year of active purchasing, we bought more than 54 properties. It sounds easy when I write those words now but it was, in fact, a little more complicated.

We started buying in the same way as many people do - putting in a deposit for every property and then getting the rest on a mortgage. As you'd expect, we were soon running out of money, so we re-mortgaged my parents' house and also my house in Widdrington, which we ended up renting rather than selling.

I also started sourcing properties, it was a way to make some money (great) but it also meant that when an estate agent rang about a property, I could see it and hopefully sell it, keeping the estate agent happy and not wasting their time.

I ended up sourcing over 100 properties for investors across the country in the first 18 months, which all came about by two posts on the Singing Pig forum (strange name, but it was a property-related website that was very popular before Facebook).

I learned through the forums and other websites about a strategy that people were using down south to buy and re-mortgage instantly. It involved a closed-bridging finance for 24 hours, buying the property on the bridge and then instantly re-mortgaging the day after for full market value (the mortgage had been arranged prior to bridging).

It meant, for instance, I would buy a three-bed house for £61,000 and instantly got a valuation for £92,000. This subsequently resulted in a mortgage of £78,200, a house with no money in and a cheque for £17,200 to spend how I wanted (it actually went into more properties, deposits and refurbs).

I was completing on two or three properties some weeks and having cheques lying around the place totalling over £50,000 that I had forgotten to cash. It was a strange time, where pounds just became numbers.

I left the hospital in 2008, which was too early really. I never bought 54 properties a year again because the thought of working there forever, that pain that made me work so hard had gone. I had become soft.

I was driving a Rover 100 at the time (it was a Metro shape but had been badged as the 100) that I bought from the local scrap yard for £700, with a three-speed automatic. Bits used to fall off it as I drove down the A1 to and from work.

The first time it happened, it felt as thought the car was going to be falling to bits right there and then.

I thought it could be the brakes, they had come away and that I was going to die. I slowly limped home and the next day took it to the garage and found it was a heat shield on the exhaust.

Relieved, I continued driving it, the car not being worth the time or effort to replace the bit of metal. The problem was the other bits would to fall off the car too.

I now knew the drill; test the brakes and give the steering a wiggle and carry on going. The exhaust fell off once, just outside the hospital, so I parked up and went and picked it up, hoping to get it welded back on. I had to replace it but a new exhaust cost a full £45.

It wasn't until I was going to a viewing that the car finally took its last trip. I was viewing a property in Blyth and outside it there was an especially high kerb.

As is the norm, I went onto the kerb and thought nothing of it. But on the trip home, other cars were flashing me, thinking they were warning me of danger ahead, I slowed down and eventually parked the car at home.

The next day my mother asked me why my car looked so strange. The suspension had broken going onto the kerb and I had one side almost on the floor and the other looking like it was a 4x4.

By this point, I had just about left my job and I was struck by the desire for a new car, but also the need to 'prove' I had made it.

My instinct was to get another run-around, but I then thought about buying something a little better that would be more reliable - a three-year-old A4 or something of that ilk.

It would be a step-up and then the next time I could get something much better.

My father advised me that I should just get the good car now, otherwise I could be waiting years. The other thing was we didn't know how long the property good times were going to last, and there was no guarantee that we would have enough money to buy a really good car down the line. (little did I know property would pay me well year after year)

So I bought a Porsche Boxster. I wasn't too sure about the open top driving, but I agreed a price and went along there with a carrier bag of cash to seal the deal.

The biggest shock came when I filled the car with £20 of fuel and two days later it was empty. In the course of driving around my home town, I used to put in £27 into the Rover Metro and drive to 30 mile round to Newcastle six days a week. I learnt that driving a Porsche was going to be much more expensive.

One thing the Porsche did was put a smile on my face every time I drove it, with the engine behind me just purring away.

So I handed all of the properties to a letting agent to look after and thought I would retire at the grand old age of 29 years and one month. I would get a tan (in my open top car) and see what I wanted to do with my life. Six weeks later, I was bored!

I also discovered that the agent wasn't doing what they should have been doing (to put it mildly) and I went from bringing in more than £20,000 a month to just £3000.

It wasn't even enough to cover the mortgages, so after some to-ing and fro-ing, I took all of the properties back. I also ended up taking one of the agency's employees with me, who became my first member of staff.

Things developed and I got a shop and opened my first office on the last

Wednesday of September 2008. Yes, you are correct, this was right at the beginning of the world's biggest recession.

I had gone into the letting business thinking 'how hard can it be? (but maybe how that went is for another book!)

Contents

1. Intro

Hello, my name is Paul Baldry and welcome to Thirty Days to Property Success. First of all, I would like you to immediately dismiss the idea that property is complicated, or hard, or you need some exceptional skills that only a few possess; or even worse that you are born with it.

I want you to discard these myths once and for all.

You do not need to come into property with any exceptional skills other than an open mind and a willingness to learn.

You will find that property is a relatively uncomplicated way to make money and change your life. Property is a straightforward process in as much that the complicated work is automatically done by solicitors and mortgage brokers. The really technical 'stuff' goes on in the background, so you are left with the pleasant money-making tasks of finding your properties, getting them for the best price and then finding even more. Rinse and repeat.

I'm not for a minute suggesting that property will not test you, stretch you or give you a curve ball every now and again - but it sure beats working for a living!

Throughout the chapters of this book, I will attempt to take you through the process of finding, negotiating a deal, getting the right team together and then renting out your property.

Your daily training will guide you through the maze of things you need to do and know about property, so much so that most people are too daunted to even start, and replace that with an easy-to-follow system.

I will take you through finding your why, thinking about your perfect day, getting your profit postcode locked down, so that you can move on to profiting from property rather than going around and around and not getting anywhere.

This course is for beginners and experienced investors alike as I include simple chapters with templates and videos that will take you through every step and help you build a solid foundation for your future success.

That solid foundation will allow you to build a strong business that can support you and your family in the life that you really want to lead. This could be supporting your income or replacing income, it could be giving you the big house, the shopping and the holidays.

It could even give you the opportunity and freedom to travel or live wherever you choose, but you must take action and put the basics in place so that you will achieve the massive success that is within your grasp.

Make the commitment today to follow through on every one of the tasks that will be presented to you over the next 30 days.

Today's task is all about making sure you understand what you will be working for.

What all the time and effort you will put into property give you in return?

And you will find out for yourself what your perfect day will look like, and you will know it has all been worth it.

You will end up in the country you dream of, and in the place that makes you feel relaxed and happy.

You will be with the people that make you fulfilled

Just pause for a moment and imagine in your mind exactly what that would look like.

That is your first task – and please use the template below for guidance – to really see your perfect day.

Go to Property30.co.uk to download this template and the rest from this book!

This is the perfect day of ......

I am in the country of....

I am living in...

I am with...

My day starts....

I am looking forward to....

I am happy because...

2. Finding your area - Profit Postcode

Today we are going right to the heart of what every investor needs - finding your own investment area. This is one of the most important things you can do and it will also be the hardest thing to 'lock down' but it will make your life so much easier once you have done it.

As an investor, you do not need to be an expert on the whole of the country. You see television experts that talk about the property market in general, but they don't know what's happening this minute in your town or city.

You don't need to know the market conditions in Liverpool, Devon, Newcastle and Edinburgh if your patch is a small town in Yorkshire!

Your area will be somewhere you know or somewhere close – preferably both.

Your area does not need to be big - a workable area is no more than 10,000 properties, but we will work a small section of this area – about 2000 - to start off with, and then expand as you hone your skills.

My patch in the north east of England consists of 10,000 properties which I split into five smaller areas that I leaflet drop once every five weeks. I did this consistently – consistency is so important.

That consistency and the other strategies I'll cover meant I was able to buy 54 properties in 12 months and I sourced over 100 properties in 18 months. And the long game can pay off. Someone came into my office last year who wanted to sell their property. They were holding one of my leaflets that had dropped through their letterbox SIX YEARS earlier.

This particular leaflet had been dropped repeatedly over a period of two years. That's the power of working one area and being consistent.

So, these are the questions you need to start asking about your patch...

Where does your area start and where does it end?

What type of properties are in your area?

What type of tenants you will be dealing with? Are they going to be students, housing benefit recipients, blue-collar workers or professionals?

What are the prices – both purchase price and rental prices? (note: don't be using Rightmove listings for your prices), use Nethouseprices or Mouseprice to get sold comparables, also known as comps.

What are the rents? What is the lowest price paid for a rental property in your area and the highest price?

How does the nicer end of your patch differ – on both rent and purchase price – from the cheaper side? (some areas are just untouchable so don't chase the very bottom of the market).

What difference would a new kitchen and bathroom make to the rental value of the property? It may be an unnecessary expense if it doesn't improve yield.

What regulations are there – blanket licencing, HMO, Article 4, or do you need to be an accredited landlord?

Will your equity come from buying at a discount or is it from refurbishing the property? – preferably it would be both.

This is not an exercise that will take you 20 minutes, but neither should it take you three months.

It is also something that will evolve over time and so you should be looking at prices and looking for trends in prices so you can pick up deals that others who are not so knowledgeable about your patch will miss.

These deals that others simply don't see because they don't have the knowledge you'll gain from reading this book could be putting £5000, £10,000 or even £20,000 in your pocket.

Over time you should be able to tell me what the price would be to buy a property on every street on your patch and what the rent is to the exact penny almost.

I have put a template together to help you research your shortlisted areas for sold prices and rental income averaged by property size and by postcode.

This may take a few days to do but it is of massive importance because when you lock down the area you invest in, and more importantly the areas that you do not invest in, you now have a patch to call your own that you can profit from - your Profit Postcode.

So, put together a brief list of areas and do a sheet for each one.

Don't be overwhelmed, just start doing a little each day.

Now go to Property30.co.uk to download your Postcode Profit sheet.

Go to Rightmove or Zoopla and search you postcode and only 1 bedroom size, list by cheapest first, then enter the prices of 10 properties you would buy. Do the same for rentals. Do each bedroom size in the postcode

Profit Postcode

Property Size (for your investment strategy Eg 1, 2, 3, 4

	________	Rental	________	Rental	________	Rental	________	Rental
1								
2								
3								
4								
5								
6								
7								
8								
9								
10								
Total								
Average								
Yield								

Please note - total is 1 through 10 added together * Average is 'Total divided by 10 * Yield is average monthly rent / average price * 1200

3. Strategies that work in your profit postcode area

Now you really need to consider what kind of tenants you want to fill your properties. So many people research the perfect area, where it is and the number of properties and the yield/capital appreciation, but a property without tenants (unless you are flipping, that is selling the property for a profit) is not an asset – it's a liability. And that liability will mean you are paying the mortgage/rent and council tax and insurance etc. until you do find a tenant.

So tenants are all important – they pay the money to pay the bills and pay you to live the life you want.

There are several things you need to consider when you're looking for tenants:

You have to establish what sort of major businesses, industries or organisations that can draw potential tenants to you are in your area?

So, the large factory with a strong, stable workforce of people that often live locally - paint factories, foundries or hospitals would come under this category.

The major draws for potential tenants would be a college and university or commuter infrastructure of a train or underground station for people who can't live right in the centre but need to get to the city. Easy access to transport will give you a steady stream of applicants.

You also have to consider the type of properties in your proposed patch – who do they appeal to? Do you want to deal with that type of tenant?

For example, if you don't want to deal with students then don't buy a five-bed property right next to a university.

And be careful not to buy a property in a low demographic area with high unemployment unless you are happy to rent to housing benefit recipients. Incidentally, more than half of my tenants are unemployed and receiving what's called now LHA – Local Housing Allowance which is now being converted to Universal Credits.

The key question you have to ask yourself is 'Can I rent the property quickly and to 'good' tenants? This essentially boils down to – are there enough tenants looking for 'your' property.

You might know most of these answers if you are looking for properties in an area very close to you, but it's always worth doing the checks no matter how familiar you are with the environment.

Start your mission by looking on 'Rightmove' or 'Zoopla' at all the rental properties available in your shortlisted Profit Postcode areas. Check how many bedrooms they have and how long they have been advertised for.

Next, go to Google Maps and check for local train stations, universities and hospitals. Also look for industrial areas and larger building works on these sites.

Then, contact letting agents and estate agents for advice about the market and the good rental areas. But be careful not to take the advice of just one. Be aware that they have a vested interest in you buying or renting from them. As a bonus, as you ring the agents be open to finding the ones who seem to be on your wavelength and could potentially bring you future deals.

Then (and this is a crucial step) go and visit the area. See it, walk down the street and sit in a coffee shop or cafe and have a drink and observe who passes.

Walk the residential streets where the properties you will be controlling are, rather than just the shopping areas. If you can go back to the residential area later in the evening, you will see how the population act after dark. If you feel comfortable in those areas, you will be comfortable having a very valuable asset left there for years to come.

Only now will you check how much demand there is for the accommodation unit. You will need to do a test advert or what are commonly called 'dummy' adverts. These are done to test the potential rental demand for any particular property, so do it before you commit to a purchase or spend money on mortgage applications or surveys.

And if you're looking to do a rent-to-rent deal (more on this later) you really need to assess tenant demand before signing a long-term rental agreement, which would include paying for any repairs.

If you would like to use one of my adverts to display at your local newsagents, just head over to Property30.co.uk to download example adverts and keep checking as I will update these all the time. It is a very basic ad but has proven very effective, and there are adverts that can also be used on Gumtree (gumtree.com) or Spareroom (spareroom.com), if you are looking to rent a property out by the room.

We've covered a lot in today's training, so maybe re-read to it and maybe make notes and then put these proven methods into practise with your shortlist of Profit Postcode areas.

4. Working through a deal

Today is a very special day, as I am going to talk you through how to analyse a deal. Well, two deals in fact - one a buy-to-let and the other a rent-2-rent deal.

You are free to do whichever is more relevant to you, or you can do both to test your ability on working your way through potential deals.

This exercise is about looking at a property and understanding what the numbers will be, so you can see potential in a property. And I'll teach you how to move quickly and efficiently so you can move on to great deal after great deal.

Don't worry if you're not into your numbers or that side of the business is 'not' your thing. It's not so hard – really, it's not!

I have seen some students creating massive spreadsheets so they can calculate everything and translate this onto graphs. Others do the absolute minimum – sold comps and yield.

On the other hand, I've seen people buying a property without ever checking the achievable rental until after they have bought it. Clearly that is not the way to build a profitable business.

Even if it works on the first property there's no guarantee that their luck will hold on the next deal or the one after that.

It's like playing Russian Roulette with your livelihood.

So, whether you are already really confident about working the numbers or it's really scary, download the deals and go through them yourself.

And when you have finished, send over your answers to deal@ Property30.co.uk.

To download, go to Property30.co.uk website (the answers are there too).

Buy To Let Deal

The property is worth £145,000 (3 comparable at that price or more)

You have negotiated a £22,000 discount

Purchase costs of £2,000

Stamp Duty of ???

Refurbishment Costs: £3,500

You need to put down a deposit of 25%

Your mortgage has an interest rate of 4.5%

Rent rental income will be £695

If you wish to use a letting agent they will charge 12%

Question Time:

What % discount have you achieved?

What is the gross yield?

What is the yield on capital introduced?

What is the net income per month / per year?

Does the deal stack up?

Now post your answers on Property30 Group

Rent-2-Rent Deal

The property is already a licenced 6 bed HMO

Landlord has retire but wishes to sell the property in 5 years time

You can rent a property for £900 increasing by £50 each year

There is £1,200 in repairs and redecoration

There is a small amount of furniture needed at a cost of £1,000

The room rent you charge is £400 including bills PCM

The cost of bills will be £500 PCM

Your annual void will be equivalent of 2 months of a room

Question Time:

What the difference in rent after costs?

What is the yield after all costs?

How long will it take to recover your initial costs?

Recalculate the above if you converted one of the living rooms into a bedroom?

What is the return over 5 years?

Is this a good deal?

5. Reviewing your financial status

Your credit file is your open wallet on full display to the world. It contains the information companies use to judge your ability to pay back debt and to make a decision on whether or not to lend to you.

In the world of property investment, you will need to, more often than not, have access to lending for mortgages, loans, trade accounts and possibly credit cards.

The way the companies check your credit worthiness is by noting how you conducted yourself with previous companies, your current mortgage and how you interact with your personal bank account.

With regards to any store cards or credit cards you may have, potential lenders will not only be checking to see if you have been regularly clearing your monthly balance on time (or made minimum payments) but also keeping track of the percentage of the balance that you are using.

If you have a credit card with a £3,000 limit and you have already spent £2,800 of that, it means that you are using 93% of your available credit, so you are almost stretched to the limit with very little buffer or room for manoeuvre.

On the flip side, having a credit card that is never used is also a 'red light' warning sign to lenders. They will interpret that as you not really needing the card, or not having the required funds to clear your monthly balance. They may assume that if you ever do start using the card, it could potentially push you over the limit financially.

So here are some very important do's and don'ts when it comes to successfully applying for mortgage finance:

Don't apply for any other lending just before applying for a mortgage. All searches leave a 'footprint' on your credit file – other companies won't be able to tell whether you have been turned down for the finance, or you simply decided not to go ahead and accept the offer. They'll also have no idea if you have taken out a sizeable loan with another company that affects your affordability for a mortgage.

Don't have a credit card with a large balance outstanding – unsecured lending is not great, especially at the high rates for credit cards.

Don't have a credit card that you don't use – either use it and pay it off each month (so you don't incur interest) or close the account.

Do pay off loans – having additional loans is expensive and puts you on the back foot for other lending applications. Get them paid off and if you have more than one loan, get the smallest one paid off first to minimise the number of loans you have.

Do always pay direct debits on time – this is a no-brainer. When you miss a payment, then it will show up on your credit file for all to see for two years. It will also reveal just how many payments you've missed and the specific amount you didn't pay back on time. This could prevent you from getting any further loans, or lock you out of getting the best rates for loan applications that are accepted.

Do check your credit file – Because it is updated from all the companies that you deal with; your file can potentially have lots of random or untrue information. You need to check all three credit referencing companies, Experian, Equifax and CallCredit. As I've mentioned previously, I had 73 errors on my file with Experian file.

Fortunately, they were all corrected within a few weeks, but it could have cost me a mortgage application.

Think before leasing a car – It seems a wonderful way to get a nice new car for a small monthly payment or a prestige car for a fixed payment BUT remember that a PCP or Personal Contract Purchase will go onto your personal credit report in full, so that Audi Q7 at £65,000 that you only paid £500 up front for, and £600 per month, has a £20,000 GFV (this it the payment you will need to make at the end to buy the car). So, you will show a personal unsecured debt of £65,000 on day one that will never go under £20,000 until you hand the car back or find £20,000 to pay off the loan at the end!

So, beware of taking out debt on new shiny things that will cost you money rather than put money in your pocket… at least until you are really making the money!

Now register with Noddle.co.uk to check your credit file, it's a free service and it will give you all the same information that the paid-for services provide.

Do it now!

6. What should I do if I have debts?

Ok, so you have some debt, most people do and it's easy to obtain and now it's going to be your job to replace 'bad' debt with 'good' debt. To do that, follow this plan:

1. Make a list of all your debts – you need to know where you are before you know where to go.

2. Go through all of your outgoings and make a decision on what can be cut. If your mobile phone is costing you £50 per month, contact the company and see if you can change it to sim-only after the first (normally) 24 months. This can be a quick and uncomplicated way to save money.

3. Use the extra money to pay off your debts. Some people would advise you to pay off the loans with the highest interest payments first. However, I would advise you to pay the smallest debts first. Don't forget to keep up the minimum payments on everything else though.

Lets say you have 2 debts to pay off

1. The first is a loan for £500 at 7% APR
2. The second is a credit card debt of £1500 at 29.9% APR

Let's assume you have an additional £200 per month spare to pay off these debts.

Which one would you pay off first?

(I would pay the lower interest, but smaller loan first so you feel like you have achieved something. This spurs you on to continue to pay of the next smallest debt)

4. DON'T USE your credit card for any day-to-day spending.

5. Once you're out of debt, don't get back into bad habits!

Now you're out of debt I would say you should have at least £1,000 saved in a separate bank account (preferably with another bank) so that you have a reserve of cash. Once this is done, I would set up a standing order to build this fund up to a level where it can cover three to six months' worth of your total bills. You could even go further than this - I've seen many sensible people with 12 months' worth of 'bill-paying' money saved.

This is not the money you will dip into to purchase a holiday or a car, but it might be used to pay for a new washing machine should your current one break unexpected. Of course you will top the account back up to its previous level as quickly as possible!

Just a quick word about Bad Debt Vs. Good Debt –

My parents once told me that all debt is bad. Well, it is and it isn't.

Debt for cars, boats, holidays, clothes, shoes, going out or spur-of-the-moment purchases is BAD DEBT.

Buying any asset that will increase in value or better still increase in value AND give you a residual income is GOOD DEBT.

The power of property is that it can give you all of the following:

- Capital appreciation
- Residual income
- Improvement uplift
- Somewhere to live (if needed)
- A leveraged asset

This last point is the really big one for me. When it comes to shares or most other forms of trading, you need to buy the asset outright and then make an income from that position.

Property is different in that you can borrow against the value of the property from Day One but make a return on the full value of the property.

For 20 to 30% deposit down and a mortgage for the rest, you collect 100% of the income (less the normally fixed mortgage payment) and 100% of the capital appreciation.

Property is one of the few investments where companies are happy to lend you the lion's share of the purchase price as they know property on the whole is a very sound investment.

Safe as houses. Anyone?

So the way property multiplies your investment is that a bank or mortgage company will lend you 70% or even 80% of the price of the property and your return, after mortgage repayments, is 100% of the full property rental income and capital appreciation.

This is a leveraged investment at work and is amazing at allowing you to make more and build your wealth.

A final point here. Section 24, which covers 'mortgage interest rate relief', is muddying the waters somewhat but, at the time of writing buying within a limited company, circumvents this issue. A chat with a good accountant is always a clever idea especially if you are a higher-rate taxpayer from other sources of income.

Catch-up and 'ask me anything'

Today we will slow things down a notch. It will be easy-going for anyone who has completed all the trainings so far, but as I have given you quite a bit of work this week, I don't want people being left behind.

So, with that in mind, I thought a day to catch up and go over your perfect day, your Profit Postcode, and the strategies and templates you will use would be of benefit.

I also wanted to give you an added bonus - as a 'thank you' for joining the training.

I want you to ask me any question you have about property and I'll personally answer it for you live on 'Property Trainer Group'.

So, between 6pm to 7pm on the first Sunday of every month- I will answer your questions.

Don't worry if you can't get to your computer between 6 and 7 o'clock. You can still post up your questions and I'll answer them either before or during the live training.

So, if you have a burning question or a deal you are looking at then bring it on and I can talk you through it.

Go to Facebook group Property30 to post your questions and get answers from myself, Andy and the team.

7. Telling people what you do

Today I'm going to focus on an easy task that a lot of people find really difficult.

The task is to tell people what you do – that's family, friends, colleagues and strangers.

Before you make a run for the hills, you are not trying to pitch to anyone, or trying to sign them up to anything.

But still, this is a really challenging thing to start doing. If you work as an accountant or mechanic and someone asks you what you do, you'll reply "I'm an accountant" or "I'm a mechanic".

You would do it without thinking – and without you worrying that you shouldn't tell people what you do.

So why should property investing be any different? By not telling everyone what you do, you are closing the door to loads of opportunities for either money or deals.

You can also allow others to put the word out to people who are looking for your services. This is massively more powerful than you talking about yourself because it's a recommendation and a validation of you as a person.

People you know will talk to people you don't know - and may never, ever meet - and bring deals and opportunities that you could never find on your own.

So your task for today is to put a post on Facebook so your family and friends can see it.

For example, you could post the following on your wall:

I'm amazed at how many opportunities are coming to me from property at the minute. I can't believe how far I've moved in such a short space of time!

Amend the wording of the above in any way you see fit but don't change it too much. And remember to make it positive because you are a positive person.

Now, to recap, remember to tell people what you do EVERY TIME someone asks.

We will revisit this later in the month, by which time you will have honed your skills in the fields of talking to people and networking.

Add to your Facebook profile

I 'm amazed at how many opportunities are coming to me from property at the minute. I can't believe the direction I'm travelling in such a short time!

Amend as required but make sure its positive and not selling.

8. Setting goals

Setting goals is so very important because it allows you to plan the results you want and keeps you on track. You'll be familiar with the motto "fail to prepare - prepare to fail."

I truly believe that by the very act of setting out your goal, you are at least 50% down the road to achieving that very goal.

I will now point you towards an extract from What They Don't Teach You in the Harvard Business School by Mark McCormack which clearly demonstrate the power of goal setting.

"This was a fascinating study conducted on the 1979 Harvard MBA program where graduate students were asked "have you set clear, written goals for your future and made plans to accomplish them?" The result, only 3% had written goals and plans, 13% had goals but they weren't in writing and 84% had no goals at all. Ten years later, the same group was interviewed again and the result was absolutely mind-blowing.

The 13% of the class who had goals, but did not write them down was earning twice the amount of the 84% who had no goals. BUT 3% who had written goals were earning, on average, ten times as much as the other 97% of the class combined! While this study only looks at earnings to quantify success, I still find it to be an extremely motivating example of why creating clear and measurable goals and writing them down is a key to success.

Feeling motivated? Here are four simple steps towards creating clear and measurable goals that will lead you to enormous success.

This will continue from the perfect day task on day 1 but will go into more detail about how you can achieve your goals - the specific things you need to do and exactly how you will do them.

From now on, choose to be among the most successful people in the world and write down your goals. Create a vision for what you want, turn that vision into a list of measurable targets, set benchmarks and celebrate your successes along the way.

By setting your goals out and writing them down, you are sending it out into the worldwide ether, if that is something you are inclined to believe in.

What you definitely will be doing (and this has been proven by scientists) is creating connections in your brain that are aligning your subconscious with your ultimate goals. Either way, it's is a strong pull towards positive results.

There's a download available at Property30.co.uk that will give you more information on setting written goals. That's today's task.

Create a Vision

The first step towards creating a goal is figuring out exactly what you want. If you don't know what you want, you won't know what you need to achieve to get there. This is actually the fun part. You get to dream. What do you really want to create for yourself? What does your ideal life look like? Don't be afraid to think big. Take 15 minutes and document your vision. Take note of the details. What does your day look like? Where are you living? Try to incorporate all of the five senses in your vision to make it most effective. What do you see, hear, smell, taste and feel throughout this ideal day?

Make it Measurable

Take your vision and turn it into a written list of concrete goals. If in your ideal world you are working for yourself, one of your goals might be to start your own company. Choose an achievable time frame to accomplish your goals, as well as measurable details, so you know exactly when you've achieved them. What exactly does it mean to start your own company? Make sure to set yourself up for success by creating goals that are realistic and achievable in the given time-frame.

Set Benchmarks

Most of our goals are a conflation of small achievements, sometimes even years of many small successes. Break your goals into small actionable steps and assign realistic time frames to each. Continue to chunk big steps into smaller and smaller steps until goals seem less daunting and achievable. Benchmarks are a great way to keep you on track. You may find you are moving more quickly or more slowly than you expected. That's not a problem, you can adjust! Adjust your expectations and timeline as you gather more information while achieving your benchmarks.

Celebrate Your Success

I believe the most important part of goal-setting is celebrating our successes. How will you reward yourself for hitting your benchmarks along the way? How will you celebrate once you've reached your goal? As we journey towards the realisation of our goals, it's important to remember our vision. Why we want something can provide us with the motivation and determination to continue to work towards it even when things don't go as planned or are more difficult than we anticipated.

GOALS

Personal
1.
2.
3.
4.

Financial
1.
2.
3.
4.

Business
1.
2.
3.
4.

Just screen shot the goals and then add as your background on your phone. I have just one on the last screen so I can read the goals, but every time I open my phone I subconsciously take in the goals.

Also print it out and put it on your fridge, next to the bed, next to the bathroom sink, at work. Inside the front cover of your diary...you get the idea!

9. Business cards/website

Today is all about how to best get your message to the outside world, so primarily you'll need a website and a business card.

The most important things to be aware of are:

You will spend longer than necessary to do it.
You will spend more time than anyone else looking at them.

Any advertising that is 80% perfect but is complete and is ready to be used is better than going for total perfection and waiting another three months. You want to be able to supply any potential customer with all the details they need immediately, rather than having to scrabble around for a piece of paper and a pen (that works!).

So, make sure you don't lose out on any tasty deals, while also being perceived as amateurish, by working on your business card for months, or putting off getting them delivered until you find the design that is 'just right'.

If you are reading this in the morning then you can have your business card designed and sent to the printers by the end of the day. Why put it off?

You only need to print 50 or 100 initially, and you can edit and upgrade as you move forward.

As for a website, a week is all you need to write the text, which you then forward to someone to build the site. Use PeoplePerHour (peopleperhour.co.uk) or similar companies for a few hundred pounds.

Regarding the words for your site, well there are only so many ways to describe what you need in the world of property. Thousands of people before you have created successful property websites, so a quick search on Google would be a good starting point.

I would suggest you read five to ten of your favourite property websites, and I'm not saying you copy their words, but instead 'take inspiration' from these websites. As long as your site isn't too similar in words or design to an existing one, then you will be fine. Let's be honest, give it a few weeks of your site being up, and others will be 'taking inspiration' from you as well.

So, decide if you need a business card and website or one without the other and get it done as quickly as possible.

10. Networking

Property is a people business and as such you need to be out there talking to people. Networking is the best way to get your name out there.

But it's not only a way to 'get out', it's also a key step towards making connections and getting your public face out to people you have not met, as well as building stronger connections with the people you have already met.

Networking can take many different forms. It can be part of a formal event or a casual get-together. It can take place in a hotel events room or a pub or bar. It could be a meal (breakfasts and lunches are common) but the important fact is you will be around people who are motivated to help each other out.

Don't be frightened about going to events - everyone was a networking newbie at some point in their journey. Every person you meet will be helpful and considerate

Remember people go to networking events to learn and meet new people - so everyone will be interested in you. You are fresh blood after all!

Here are a few rules for you if you haven't been to an event before (or maybe even if you have).

1. Be interested in others - ask questions before telling them what you do

2. Don't try to sell to everyone when you first meet them

3. Don't ever go around the whole room and just hand your business card to every person - This is not BNI (or maybe it is a BNI event!)

4. Only give cards to people who you speak to and it has become apparent that you can help them and they can help you.

I often take only three business cards to an event so I can laser-focus my decision on who to hand them out to.

Also, listen carefully to all the speakers and take notes. I was at the Berkshire Property Meet* a few years ago and getting there late, I had to sit right at the back. Bummer, right? Well, not exactly. I looked to my left and sitting just two seats away from me was one of the biggest names in property investing. You'd imagine someone of that status would think they knew it all, but I observed him scribbling down more than eight pages of A4 notes! I'd never seen anyone take so many notes in my life.

There is always so much more to learn, so I want you to find a minimum of two events within the next four weeks. Book yourself onto them and GO to the event - just do it. You definitely won't regret it.

* A long-established and very popular networking event that has since closed.

11. Organising your time

Your time is your most valuable asset. Money comes and goes, your new car ages and rusts, the Mulberry handbag gets scuffed and marked - but you can always get more of them. They are a commodity that can be saved for later.

Time is different. It is something that even when it's not being used it is being used. Think about it.

Watching TV, playing on Candy Crush and incessant checking of Facebook all use up time that could be used constructively towards fulfilling your ultimate goal of being financially free.

No, I'm not saying that you should never do anything that is fun or frivolous with your time, but understand that no one I have ever met has ever told me they wished they had spent more time playing games on their iPhone. However, plenty of people have told me they wished they had got into property earlier.

Some rules to organise your time. Start by working out what you spend your time on. Today's download is the activity Tracker (check Property30.co.uk to download) and use it for the next two weeks.

When I did this very first time, I had a personal revelation about how much time I spent doing things that were neither constructive nor producing a profit. Think of it as a dieter tracking their food so as to wean them off the sugary sweets that give them no benefits at all.

Second, you need to organise your day so that all the important tasks are locked into your diary. This could be working around travel, your job, children and other commitments. You should make the best, most productive use of your time, and you can always do things like checking out Rightmove on your laptop or smartphone during your train or bus journey to work, follow up any leads during your lunch break and fulfil any appointments before heading back to your home life.

You could also book in an hour after you've put your children, if you have any, to bed so that you can complete any follow-ups with vendors and estate agents. In most cases, this would be done via email.

By booking your appointments into on a fixed diary like this, you are less likely to get distracted by new tasks or other commitments.

The next stage in effective time management is to use NET time – which stands for No Extra Time. This is effectively dead time that you can use for work.

Examples would include standing in a queue in a bank or getting a haircut. Never drive long distance if you can get the train or be driven as these hours can be used much more effectively.

I get a lot of work done while travelling across the country in the First Class compartments of trains. A small extra cost to your ticket gives you free Wi-Fi, drinks and food so you can concentrate on your business and making more money.

So, your task for today and for the next two weeks is to track your time either using the template provided or using notes on your phone or computer (See below)

Twice an hour, you can write just one word about what you were doing in the previous 30 minutes. If you cannot describe what you were doing as productive work, then enter in capitals 'NOTHING'. At the end of the day you can tally up all the time you spent on unproductive tasks.

I'm sure that by the end of the second week you will have fewer wasted half hours as you train your brain to be constantly thinking 'should I be doing this or could I be doing something better?'

So, today's task will take some effort but the returns massively outweigh the commitment. Please trust me on that.

Go to Property30.co.uk to download your copy of the Time Tracker.

Weekly Time Tracker

	Monday	Tuesday	Wednesday	Thursday	Friday	Saturday	Sunday
7.00							
7.30							
8.00							
8.30							
9.00							
9.30							
10.00							
10.30							
11.00							
11.30							
12.00							
12.30							
13.00							
13.30							
14.00							
14.30							
15.00							
15.30							
16.00							
16.30							
17.00							
17.30							
18.00							
18.30							
19.00							
19.30							
20.00							
20.30							
21.00							
21.30							
22.00							

12. Advertising/Leaflets/Posters

Advertising is the lifeblood of any business and yours is no different. It's probable you might only need to buy or control a few properties to give you the profits that you require. But, all the same, you need to be getting potential deals coming to you via networking, contacts you already have and estate agents.

But more often than not, you'll get your leads through direct marketing - leaflets, vendor/landlord letters, shop posters and boards, newspaper adverts and websites, taxi cards, takeaway menus, bin stickers, billboards large and small; as well as Facebook groups and advertising, plus many, many more methods.

What you need to decide is where and how you are going to advertise. If you do a one-off advert in one medium, you're not going to get a lot of calls – so you need to be consistent and frequent across a variety of platforms.

So, I have created a template that will allow you to examine the multitude of options open to you, and also give you the opportunity to brainstorm some ideas of your own.

Here I'll go through some of the most popular options, in turn.

Leaflets are the bread and butter of any marketing strategy. They are cheap to print (one penny or less each) and you can target areas that have the kind of properties you want. I do sometimes get people contacting me from outside the area I drop in after they either see the leaflet at a friend's house or the number is passed on to them by someone else.

The leaflets do need to be dropped and I always do the posting personally when I am leafleting a new area the first time, so I can be on the ground and observe what the properties are like.

If you are time-rich but cash-poor then this may be something that you will continue to do until you get some deals under your belt. Otherwise, you'll need to get someone else to deliver leaflets.

I had my own leafleter and it worked out really well but I had to kiss a lot of frogs to get to that stage. I now use small leafleting companies as they are more accommodating than larger companies when you're only ordering 2000 per week and I am flexible enough to allow them to deliver them on any day within a seven-day period. I never allow them to double up one week if they've been too busy the previous week. I give them consistent, regular work and that should be respected both ways.

Vendor/Landlord letters – This is such an under-used technique to get your leaflets in front of the right people at the right time. Think about it, if you send a leaflet just after the landlord has rented the property they won't be interested – but do it when the property has been empty for a month and they might just give you a call!

So, to find properties that are within your target market, use boards outside properties - that's how it used to be done. The easier, more modern way is via Rightmove and Zoopla, where you can bring up a list of properties for sale or for rent (if you are looking at lease options and r-2-r). Then put all off the properties into an Excel spreadsheet.

At this stage, you have the street and town. Now you need the door numbers and there are a few ways to obtain these.

1. Open the details on the property and click on the EPC. Some agents give the full first page - which just happens to include the full address.

2. Look for the most recent 'sold price' which will include the date, and then go to the top of the page and put your mouse over 'House prices'. You will be given a few options and you want the one which says, 'what's sold on the street name of the property'.

This brings up a list of sold properties on the same street of the property that you have open. Now scroll down to the date and match it to the price and, hey presto, you should have the door number.

3. If not, open the external picture and see if the door number is shown on the picture. Finally, if all else fails, take a drive down to the street and find the property that matches the picture on the website.

As a side note, if you are looking for HMOs, all registered HMOs are on a list and this is on the public record so you can request a copy. This will also reveal the name of the landlord. You may have to be persistent as some councils will try not to give this information to you, but they can't legally refuse. So this is a quick way to get a list to contact.

Now you have the list, you will need to arrange to send three letters at a minimum to each address and at set intervals. Again, consistency is key here like with everything else in property.

Shop poster/cards and boards are a cheap and simple way to get your details out and represent an additional touch point with your potential customers. You should place an A6 card – which is a quarter of an A4 sheet - into every newsagent, sandwich shop and café in your target area. Also, be on the lookout for any shops that have already have cards in their window.

13. Talking to vendors/landlords

Talking to vendors is a scary proposition. You start by speaking on the phone and, unfortunately, there is the potential to ruin your chances of a deal within two or three minutes if you try too hard to reach an agreement at this early stage.

The purpose of the first call should only be to take down details. It could be you personally writing down the information, someone you know doing the job for you or, better still, an answering service that can be waiting for the call. However, you set it up, make sure a script is followed. And don't put yourself in the embarrassing position of trying to take a call when you're out with the kids or shopping. This will come over as very unprofessional and could lose you the sale. Answering services, which I recommend, don't cost very much and you can implement them on a call-by-call basis.

I have attached the questions you need to complete at Property30.co.uk, so have a look and then put it into your own words. If you are going to be answering the calls yourself, make sure you put in plenty of practice so you come over in the best possible way.

The next stage is the appointment. This is where you actually go to the property and build some rapport with the vendor. The more touch points you can have, the better.

I would strongly suggest you stick to the following process:

1. Someone takes the call and takes down all of the vendor's details in the most professional manner.

2. A phone call is made to the vendor to verify all the details.

3. A text is made to confirm the appointment.

4. The appointment itself.

5. A follow-up telephone call is made to the vendor the following day.

6. A second appointment with the vendor.

This can all be done within three or four days, ideally, and by the time you've reached the last stage, you will know them and they will know you. You will have built on your trust and rapport at every stage and you will have demonstrated a professionalism that shows you take the vendor's problems seriously.

Later on in this programme, we will go into more detail about the appointment itself, but for now, get your call answering system in place as quickly as possible.

Go to Property30.co.uk to download the full vendor questions.

Questions For Vendors

Name?
Address?
Postcode?

Type of property?
Number of Bedrooms?
No. of reception rooms?

Gas central heating?
Double glazed?
Parking?

Is it on with an estate agent?
If so Which agent?
How much is the property on for?
How long been on the market

Reason for selling?

Which day can I come round to have a chat?

Don't ask!

How much do you want for the property?
If I was to offer XXX would you take it?

I do lease options...should I tell you about them? (leave until later)

Write your questions in your own style Try to outsource the call answering to a PA Service

14. Talking with estate agents

My good friend Phil Elder has kindly agreed to write a chapter about dealing with estate agents as he spent his early days working in an estate agency and is now an investor he has been on both sides of the transaction and well placed to give you the inside track on dealing with agents.

Firstly, there are two important things to remember when dealing with and approaching estate agents - firstly they are human beings and, second, please be nice!

While this may seem a little bit silly, often estate agents have a reputation as being sharks who are only out to rip you off. This false perception seems to colour people's attitudes towards them!

Also, the biggest relationship destroyer when you initially approach agents is the Billy Big Time attitude. I.e. Hi, I have loads of money. Do you want to buy cheap houses and make loads of cash? (look at me, Mr Flash!)

I can assure you that this is the quickest way to find yourself attaining 'dinner' status (meaning your details/business card gets suitably filed in the bin.

It's a little like a dating ritual where everyone should be on their best behaviour. Listen to what the estate agents has to say, rather than just talking about yourself the whole time. The key is to engage with the other person.

The relationships that you can build with the correct agents have the potential to serve you very well in your property investing career.

Whether you are simply looking to purchase a few buy to lets, or trying to acquire the whole town, the fact that agents day in and day out live and breathe property sales and lettings should make them your new go-to best friends. So they should be treated accordingly.

Little gifts of appreciation can go a very long way (and I certainly don't mean brown envelopes full of cash).

A bunch of flowers can work really well – especially if the agent is a woman! After your purchase has completed, don't forget to visit the florist and make sure their finest bouquet sits on her desk for the whole office to see.

You should remember most of the phone calls that estate agents receive are from disappointed vendors, asking why their house hasn't sold at the full asking price off the first viewing within 24 hours of the valuation taking place, so simple gestures of gratitude go a very long way!

Also, wherever possible take the time out to drop in to say hello with a coffee, a cake or some other little treat for your favourite agent. If you are at the forefront of someone's mind for the right reasons well, guess what, that's exactly when you are going to get the magic call.

Hopefully it will be along the lines of "Hi, I have the perfect property for you, so let's get you round there first before I put it to the market!"

I have actually had valuers pre- book a viewing for me the following day and told me "Hi Phil, I've just seen the perfect place for you. I've booked you in for a viewing tomorrow and the asking price is £X but the vendor will accept £y." As I'm sure you can imagine, that is a great position to be in.

Something that you always need to be clear on is fee structure. Agents are commission-driven, so while a basic salary is often in place, they don't really earn properly unless they sell!

Also, they don't get paid until the sale of that property completes, so while they are motivated to sell property, they are even more motivated to sell to people who will honour that purchase.

While first time buyers may be attractive prospects as they won't be part of any chain (i.e. the purchase won't be delayed while they wait to sell another property), they also have no mortgage history, so they may have some difficulty getting one.

As far as chains go, long ones only need one problem - somebody pulls out for any reason at all - and the sale falls through and the agent does not get paid!

I hope you can see how motivated the agents are to work with, and therefore sell to, serious and professional investors!

Even if these people are offering a little less for the property, they are a safe bet for the vendor and, often more importantly, for the agent! Knowing you will complete without any hitches will save them worrying about having to go back through the process of re-marketing the property (this costs money) more viewings (again more time and cost) and starting the process all over again (longer wait until pay day).

Here are a few simple lines to possibly add into your introduction to a new estate agent

1. "Whilst I invest myself I also work with a bank of investors"
Saying you are part of a larger group suggests there is more money behind you, and therefore the agent has the opportunity to make more

sales and more commission payments. It also suggests you are a very financially secure individual. Also, the subtle use of the word 'bank' suggests money without actually saying something like: "I have loads of cash or £X to spend. As I mentioned before, this is a bit of a turn-off.

2. "Normally we buy but demand is outstripping supply so hence we are looking at / having to…"

Great for those looking to rent 2 rents. This suggestion that you buy normally again makes them feel safe in your financial position but also install confidence in your experience! It also makes them feel comfortable that you are doing the strategy (be that HMO, SA, Corporate lets etc.) in your own properties, so if you're happy to do it in your own then it can't be that bad!

It also subtly opens up the opportunity to buy should the correct opportunity arrive – this is if you're working with agent in mixed markets - i.e. sales and lettings - and gives you the potential to look at both options.

Finally the use of "we" suggests a company or a larger organisation, therefore you look more professionally, making them feel safer and therefore the landlords safer!

3. We work with companies like (*name drop large employers in your area*) providing housing for staff

Again 'we' suggests size and security Using this method suggests that these big organisations have trust in you, so therefore why could they not look to develop trust with you as well? Please note the use of 'LIKE'. You are not saying you actually are! This information can easily be achieved from a simple search on the internet. Sites like Wikipedia etc. often state in a town's search the names of the larger employers in the area.

As a parting thought, for those who may feel a little shy about this, or are nervous of making mistakes, simply go to a town that you're not intending to invest in and try it out!

Most estate agencies tend to have offices so simply pop in give it a try. When you finish each visit, note down any objections or questions that have arisen and try adjusting your approach the next time, or at least be prepared to handle the same questions if you're asked them again. Then, once you feel more comfortable, try it on home ground!
What's the worst that could happen?

Phil Elder
www.philipelder.co.uk

Get these phrases and more in a handy download to keep in your pocket at Property30.co.uk.

15. Following up leads

Following up on leads is so important to the success you have with your viewings.

The reality is, you will get turned down more times than your offer will be accepted. That is if you are doing it right!

You should be offering on 90% plus of all the properties you view. But for every 10 offers you make, especially at estate agents, 8 will be turned down initially. This is not to say they won't take a slightly higher offer, it's just that their need is not sufficient for your very low first offer.

So you need to either decide to increase you offer or leave your offer on the table so the vendor can come back to you. But don't rely on estate agents to do this, as they are always busy and, invariably, they won't check their records properly when the vendor drops his or her price.

You need to be proactive on this and keep a small record of every property you view every week if you are direct to vendor; or monthly if you are going through an estate agent. Always make follow-up calls. Find out how the vendor is getting on and whether they have reconsidered your original offer or increase slightly over time.

Your offers should be low enough that you are buying at a discount, (don't expect discounts in London or similar areas) so that you will have equity in the property from day one. Anyone can buy at full market or over the market price, but you are a property professional, so never do this.

16. Checking Portals

The portals massively improve your ability to see all properties available in one place and in the comfort of your own home.

When I started the portals (a website where property from all estate agents is grouped onto one website) were in their infancy and you needed to go to each and every estate agent to see what they had available.

Even then, you only got the description, with gaps for pictures. The few photographs that were made available were taken with film cameras, developed and then attached to the front page using a Pritt Stick.

You did viewings on the advice of an estate agent, and you would do a lot of drive-bys to check properties ahead of every viewing.

However, nowadays you have such an amazing facility available to you in the shape of the portals, make sure you start using them to the fullness of your ability, getting everything you possibly can out of them.

Even if you are not buying properties directly from estate agents, you have unlimited access to a pool of information that is free to use.

You can immediately find out where prices are going up, prices are going down and also when more stock is available, or when things are starting to get tighter. All of this information, and a lot more, can be gleaned from portals.

If one estate agent is getting a lot of stock on, what they are doing as agents can be easily done as a deal sourcer or property buyer in your own right. This is an example of where you can copy or take inspiration from what the established professionals are doing.

So if you are using an estate agent to buy property, then you should be checking out the portals no less than once a day.

You genuinely don't need to spend a long time doing this. As you go along, you can save your searches into all three portals. That way, you don't have to look at all the dream houses that pop up that you would never, ever buy.

Use NET* time when you are travelling to work, having a break, at lunchtime or any spare five seconds you have to get on the portals, check them out to see what has become available.

This is even more important now that we have real-time advertising where the portals will instantly place an advert of a property.

So your task today is to save your searches in all three portals. Once this is done, check these searches at least once a day.

* NET time stands for 'No Extra Time'. Most people see travelling on public transport, standing in queues, running on a treadmill etc. as 'dead time' or 'me time' but you can always utilise these opportunities to check out the portals on your laptop, tablet or smartphone, or any other type of productive endeavour

* NET time stands for 'No Extra Time'. Most people see travelling on public transport, standing in queues, running on a treadmill etc. as 'dead time' or 'me time' but you can always utilise these opportunities to check out the portals on your laptop, tablet or smartphone, or any other type of productive endeavour

17. Reviewing properties online

Today is going to be a little different.

I'm going to go through how I check properties out via the portals and how, by having on-the-ground experience combined with knowledge of the property, I can find out more about property from the property sites and a cursory glance than spending time viewing properties that do not fit my criteria.

Go to the link below to access an instructional video where I'll tell you everything you need to know about finding properties online. I will talk you through all the things you need to look out for and help you understand the various heating systems, the different types of windows and how to check the roof, all without visiting the property in person.

Go to Property30.co.uk to view the full video and see what other gems of information you can pick up.

18. Carrying out viewings

Viewings are the act of going to a property and actually seeing a property this the stage when all the researching on the portals, the recommendations from estate agents and calls from adverts and leaflets come together and you arrange to see the property for yourself.

But the reality is that the 'viewing' doesn't start when you are inside the property, it starts before you see the property - done right before you even agree the appointment.

You need to get an idea of the area, the price, comps (known as comparables) and idea of the property itself. IF you are buying in one area then much of this can be streamlined as it will be repetition from previous investigation.

So first we will look at price, using Nethouseprice, Mouse Price or Rightmove sold, using the postcode to search all property that has sold in the last few years. This will give you an idea of what properties are actually selling for (rather than relying on estate agent's marketing price or vendor's over optimistic price)

Now you have an understanding of the property from the pictures and questions you asked the vendor or estate agent and know of the likely price you will pay and you have checked out the area that the property is in.

Now its time to get inside.

I have a rule in property to no matter what, start at the top and work down.

Outside

1. Chimney.
2. Roof - including ridge tiles and flashing.
3. Gutters and facias - that's the bit the gutter attaches to.
4. Check the windows and door - make sure they are all double glazed, don't just assume as advertised.
5. Walls - they should be straight and no bricks cracked or broken. In older properties, check for holes drill along the bottom 3 or 4 course of the bricks for a replacement damp-proofing.
6. Outbuildings and extensions - if they have any.
7. Finally boundary walls and the garden or yard - you are standing in, unless of course you are coming off the street and straight into the property.

Inside

1. Smell - a musty smell is damp or mildew. Find out why.
2. Ceiling - easier to see room size and check for damp patches, cracks or issues in corners of rooms.
3. Windows - frames, glass and any damp around frame (touch is good to find moisture).
4. Walls - tenants prefer properties with walls and make sure there are no cracks or issues.
5. Skirting boards - damp issues.
6. Flooring - level and no wobbles, make sure the flooring is good or account for replacement.

Other things to check

1. Boiler – check type and age.
2. Radiators – make sure they are in each room.
3. Gas and electric meters.

4. Bathroom - showers are becoming more important.

5. Kitchen - cabinets, cooker and hob, other integrated white goods and spaces for other appliances.

Your senses

1. Use your sight – always be looking for the out of place.
2. Use your nose - for smell of damp.
3. Use your hands – finding cold walls where there is damp.
4. Use your ears – loose flooring, anything that is making an unusual sound.
5. Use your balance – looking for uneven flooring and sunken floors.

Of course you will have to do this while the vendor or agent is in the property and this is also a gold mine of information about how long its been lived in, why they're moving. How long its been on the market and what has been done to the property.

So once inside the property, spend some time talking to the vendor or agent about the property and trying to find out about their experience of the property.

This is the time to build some rapport with the vendor as it will be they who will accept your offer. Sometimes you can build the rapport to a point that they will accept an offer lower than they normally would or your offer over another offer.

(This normally because you have instilled a sense that you will complete and not mess anyone around, or you can complete faster as you have finance in place and don't need to sell another property)

The more viewings you do the better and the more understanding you will have the properties you are looking to buy and can compare one property against the next both in quality but also in price.

I would suggest you are doing at least 10 viewings per week and todays task is to arrange some viewings with estate agents now.

If you want this is of what to look out for in a handy download go to Property30.co.uk to get it now

19. Control V Owning

I think one of the most important things to learn is that you don't need to own property to make money from property. You can control property to make money. Basically, this is the fundamental concept behind rent to rent (or R2R in the shorthand version).

The thing with actually owning a property is that you have also 'bought' two long-term money-making strategies, whereas 'controlling' only gives you one of these two streams.

The two income streams are rental income and capital appreciation. The latter has had a bad rap lately. If you're relying on appreciation and the rent is short of the monthly mortgage repayments and your other costs (insurances, letting fees etc.) then you're not in a good place.

So just don't ever put yourself in this position. During the last recession, which started in 2007/08, thousands of people lost their investment properties and a lot more besides because they went down the road of thinking they didn't need to worry about rental income.

However, over time property does appreciate. Take for example a standard property that is making you £200 a month in net cash-flow – or £2400 a year; over 10 years this property will have made you £24,000.

And that's your cash return for all the work, all the repairs and also taking into consideration all of the void periods. This does not even include paying management fees. After all of that, you'll be lucky to have cleared £10,000 over the course of a decade.

Now look at that very same property that's worth, say, £100,000 in today's money. Over that same 10-year span, it doubles in value to

£200,000.

So, over the same period, you've made £10,000 a year by doing absolutely nothing.

If you're doing rent-to-rent, and you've made about £2000 per year for all the work, and the owner has made £10K, then it's perfectly OK that it's skewed that way, massively in the owner's favour, because ownership is the power.

You can always swap sweat equity* for money, but wouldn't you much rather be on the owner's side of the equation?

So definitely do rent-to-rents where lucrative opportunities arise, but do try to change them to lease options** so that you can buy the properties at a future date.

Hold on to the money that you make from R2Rs so that you can build up funds to buy properties. The key message here is that you should plot for the long-term growth that ownership gives you.

The ultimate wealth for yourself and for your family is from owning assets, rather than just controlling them, and that's why I'd suggest that you should start owning properties as soon as possible.

I have attached templates containing all the above numbers, and plenty more besides, so if you prefer to see the concept represented in a more visual way, go ahead now and download the template form Property30.co.uk.

Rent-2-Rent - What you make \ What the Landlord makes

		Standard House	HMO (5 Rooms)	HMO (9 Rooms)
Rent-2-Rent				
You Rent out for		£6,000	£20,800	£37,440
minus - Landlord Rent	a	£2,400	£9,600	£17,280
minus - Costs		£400	£3,000	£6,000
minus - Voids		£300	£500	£2,000
Your Annual Profit		**£2,900**	**£7,700**	**£12,160**

Double in value from		£80,000	£180,000	£280,000
10% yearly increase in value		£8,000	£18,000	£28,000
Landlord Rent	a	£2,400	£9,600	£17,280
	Total	**£10,400**	**£27,600**	**£45,280**
Over 15Years (7.5%)		£5,333.33	£12,000	£18,666.67
Landlord Rent	a	£2,400	£9,600	£17,280
	Total	**£7,733**	**£21,600**	**£35,947**
Over 20 Year (5%)		£4,000	£9,000	£14,000
Landlord Rent		£2,400	£9,600	£17,280
	Total	**£6,400**	**£18,600**	**£31,280**

As you can see with rental income and capital appreciation that the landlord, you have rented from, achieves more income with you doing all the work! They profit from ownership, you get to profit from a property that you have rented and put little money in

* Sweat equity is contribution to a project or enterprise in the form effort and toil. In the context of property, it refers to value-enhancing improvements made to properties.

** Consult your solicitor for guidance before entering into any residential lease option agreements, especially in Scotland.

20. Legals

Today I'm going to talk about the legals relating to the buying, selling and renting of property. I'm not referring to landlord accreditation or article four licensing.

What I am talking about is if you are classed as a letting agency or an estate agency - and many people do think you need to have a High Street shop to be classed as one of these.

But if you are doing rent-to-rents, you are in effect a letting agency. You are taking someone else's property, putting third parties into it, and then making a profit from it. And that's no different from being a letting agent.

As such, in the eyes of the law, you are a letting agency.

If you are doing R2Rs, or managing other people's properties 'on the side', then you need to be registered with the property ombudsman's scheme, you must have professional indemnity insurance and if you hold data on people, then you have to be registered with the information commissioner's office.

And if you're doing deal sourcing, deal packaging or in any way selling property or deals on properties, you are classed in the eyes of the law as an estate agent by another name.

So, again you need to be registered with the property ombudsman and the other organisations referred to above. But, in addition, you need to have anti-money laundering registering.

None of this mandatory housekeeping will cost a lot. It will maybe be about £600-£700 for all of them, and it will ensure that you are fully compliant.

A quick word of advice here. When you are registering for professional indemnity insurance, tell them that you are a letting agency or an estate agent, because it is always easier to get insurance for these businesses (obviously don't hide information if asked a direct questions).

You're not hiding anything, as a High Court ruling in 2014 stated that deal packaging and all the 'we'll buy your house quickly' companies are all estate agencies by a different name. So you are using this ruling to your advantage.

Just to put your mind at rest, if you rent out properties that you personally own, then you don't need to be registered.

And, also if you buy properties from estate agents, or you are getting properties direct from vendors, as long as you are not selling these properties on to third parties, then you do not need to be registered.

I've attached a template here of frequently asked questions (FAQs) as well as other resources. Download it now, and you can find out what you need to be fully compliant in your own business

Go to Propery30.co.uk to get all the documents and updates!

Legal Requirements for Sale and Rental Businesses

(Very official title for something simple but needs to be complied with)

RENTAL

Q: What lettings/rentals needs registration?

Any property you do not own that you rent out to a third party.

Q: What businesses does this cover?

Letting agent, Rent-to-Rent

Q: What registration do I need?

You will require the following

1. Professional Indemnity Insurance
2. Property Ombudsman Membership
3. If you store data – Information Commissioner Office Registration

Q: How much does this cost?

You will be looking at approximately £600

SALES

Q: What sales need registration?

Any property you do not own that you sell to a third party.

Q: What businesses doe this cover?

Estate Agent, Deal Sourcing, Fast Sale Company (sell properties on),

Q: What registration do I need?

1. Professional Indemnity Insurance
2. Property Ombudsman Membership
3. Anti-Money Laundering Registration
4. If you store data – Information Commissioner Office Registration

Q: How much does this cost?

You will be looking at approximately £700

21. Finding tenants

Today and over the next few days, we will cover tenants - something that is not often explored in training or by gurus. But if you are not renting property and will not rent property – i.e. you are just selling deals or doing flips, then you can proceed directly to day 26.

Finding tenants is something that turns your liability - a property costing you money either on mortgage or rent – into an asset that makes money for you every month.

To get tenants, you need to get the property in front of the right people at the right time. This means taking the right pictures (which I will be covering on another day, as it is so important), putting the property on the right websites and giving it enough time to allow you to have a selection of applicants rather than just taking the first person who comes along!

So let's assume you have taken good pictures, now where do you put them? Well it depends on what the property is, where it is and how much demand there is in general for the area. Also take into account how much time you have to devote to one project, as that time could perhaps be better spent finding more properties.

The main letting agents (both online and local) allow you to advertise on Rightmove, Zoopla, OnTheMarket or a combination of all three.

You must be a letting agent to post on these sites and they are pretty expensive – for example, Rightmove costs more than £1000 per month. Letting agents will also have a list of applicants waiting to move quickly, so they could find someone straight away from their preferred list, or a person spotting a property in their shop frontage and walking into the shop to make an offer. This is something that happens more than you'd think but, of course, it only applies to local agents.

You don't need to pay a lot or have the letting agent manage the property if you want to do this yourself. A 'tenant find only' service would supply a tenant - normally credit checked and a tenancy signed with the bond and first month's rent paid. In this case, the letting agent deducts their fee and passes the remaining amount on to you.

Next would be online sites. Gumtree and Spareroom are two of the better-known ones but there are others that are more for your direct to landlord tenants - my estate agency uses these as well as the two mentioned above.

Gumtree has a strong following and can get you the applicants that other advertising will not. Also, these sites are also very good at advertising rooms to let - Spareroom is exclusively for room rents and as a site almost can't be beaten for that purpose. The sites charge a small fee per advert or you can charge monthly and do unlimited adverts if you have a number of properties.

Facebook - as Facebook has taken over the world it is also an effective way to advertise properties, either through groups (and there are specific groups for advertising properties) but also on your wall. That is especially useful if you are renting property locally – because other users will pass on your details to people whom they know are actively looking.

Next would be in newsagents and other local shops - place a small card advert in all the shops in the vicinity of the property as people 'normally' will rent within a close radius of their current property. For that reason, they will be looking in the windows of their local newsagents, corner shops or off-licences for their next home. I have used this method in the past and I had so many calls I ended up having to switch off my phone!

Other ways to attract tenants include contacting local firms, or businesses using contractors in your area. Notice boards in colleges, universities and hospitals can be good if the properties are close to those institutions and I even once leaflet-dropped a whole village as I knew tenants would only come from that village, where I had a few vacant properties to rent. It worked well and I have a steady stream of applicants from there as we are known in that place as the people to come to for property.

So where should you advertise? Start with all of the places I have mentioned. The more you advertise, the more applicants will see your property and the better selection of tenants you will have.

I would look at using some of these techniques to test new areas to gauge potential applicant levels before buying any properties.

22. Checking tenants

Today I'll walk you through the tricky task of checking applicants to make sure they are suitable for your property – i.e. making sure they are who they say they are and that they have no bankruptcy, CCJs, bad debt to landlords or other issues that would make you uneasy about supplying a property to them.

You also want to make sure they can manage to pay the rent, in full and on-time month in and month out. You want to verify this before they move in and not have to deal with problems after they are in the property and causing you hassle and costs - both non-payment of rent and the cost to remove the tenant.

Now that's enough scaremongering. Fortunately, bad tenants are fairly rare, assuming you've set up everything in the right way - especially at the beginning.

Always get any applicant to check a property before agreeing to take it, take an admin fee (although not in Scotland) as it discounts many applicants looking to get in on no money (why do they have no money? - will they have money to pay your rent).

Always get every adult to fill in an application form where they provide all the necessary details (two or three pages is fine - nothing too big). Also, make sure every applicant provides photo ID and proof of address (this discounts any criminals or people not wanting to be found).

After that, get an employers and landlord reference to verify what is on the application. Finally, check where they are living now! This takes time and effort but it will pay dividends on the long run.

If you say to an applicant "I'll come around to your property and fill in the forms" and they only let you into the kitchen and the living room, that will give you a good indication of how they live and how the children (if they have any) treat the property.

A lot of the credit checks and referencing can be outsourced either to the letting agent, or by using a credit checking service online. But the leg work of going to the applicant's property can't be outsourced.

Finally, always take a full month's rent and another full month's rent for bond. Again, this will give you some coverage if future rental payments are not forthcoming.

My own letting agency can find a tenant, manage your property or just do the referencing and credit checks for your property for a special discounted fee by using the code 'Property30' contact Clarke Holland on 01670 800 026 or email property30@clarkeholland.com.

Or if you are looking to start or expand your portfolio we do armchair investment services of 10%+ returns starting at only £15,000 investment by calling 01670 800 027

23. Communicating with tenants

Communicating with tenants can be scary. Where do you stand? Will they use everything you say against you? What if things are strained or confrontational?

Well the good news is, it's not as bad as you think. Setting boundaries at the start is important as is the application procedure - as discussed previously, having the right information off the tenants and supplying the right information to the tenants to systemise your tenant move-in - from the tenancy or AST to prescribed information for the registration of the bond.

You will also need to supply information on how to use the heating. It doesn't have to be the full manual as these often get lost or misplaced throughout the tenancy - but a scan of the manual and the print on demand or easy-to-follow description of how it all works. Save all this to your computer in a folder and have the 'hard copy' in the property ready for each tenant. This will save you time and also saves the tenant having to call you to find out how to use the system.

You can do this for the heating, cooker, fire (if it's complex), alarm (without the code itself) and anything else that could cause issues with the tenant.

It makes the tenant think that you're proactive but, from your end, it only needs to be done once and then it can be made available in minutes to every future tenant. You can outsource this task to your letting agent or even have a virtual assistant email it to your tenants so you never have to see them.

When tenants do call then - as strange as it may seem - speak to them.

I often get asked for a form or letter to send about some issue or some non-issue. I say don't worry about paperwork. You want the tenant to look after the property, pay the rent and not bother the neighbours. If they do something that is an issue then speak to them, either in person or on the phone.

This allows them to get a better idea of your tone and personality – two things that can't be put across on any of the official forms you send. Also, a quick call can sort everything out in five minutes, rather than trying to find the time to write a letter or fill in a form and then post it or drop it off - then waiting either for the issue to be resolved or their response.

It's more open and effective to deal with issues person to person. Otherwise the tenant can take the official route back or just ignore any letters - how do you even know if they have received your letter in some cases?

Forms and documents must be used at the beginning and at the end of a tenancy of course - and any official notices need to be dealt with properly, using the right forms. But with any really critical issue, I would call or hand over the documents face to face, so I could communicate as a human being what is and what is not acceptable.

I often get asked for a template form or letter, but it's best to try to talk to the tenant first. When you do need to write, an informative book to use to get sample letters is 'Landlord's Letters' by Adam Church. It will help you to get the right structure.

So if you want to speak to me – contact me on the Property30 Facebook group.

24. Collecting rent

When things do go bad with tenants, then swift action is required to put the tenancy back on course or to minimise lost rent and costs.

The way to deal with tenants differs according to the type of tenant you are dealing with.

I will talk about working tenants first and if rent is not paid, I would initially text a tenant - as they are often working during the day.

Write something like 'just wondering if payment has been made, drop me a text if it has or call me to arrange'.

If you don't get a response, then call them at a reasonable hour. If another 24 hours pass without them getting back to you, then go to the property. Get face to face with the tenant and find out if there is a problem or have they lost their job?

Can you help them to claim housing benefit or let them leave early to minimise arrears? (it can take a minimum of six months to get someone out of a property using the legal system - never mind the related stress).

Talking the tenant through their financial issues could save you from £6,000-£10,000 or more in lost rent, solicitor and court fees. If someone owes you a month's rent, can't pay and has no hope of paying -and they offer to leave in two weeks (you can't tell them they must leave - that's illegal eviction) it would only cost you a few hundred pounds. Then you can immediately find a new tenant who pays the rent, job done.

And as a bonus, the former tenant might pay you the money they owed once they have got back on their feet again (this could be because they need a reference to let another property). Or you could just write off the debt - it's your business decision.

Tenants who are not in employment are different in that you can't get an attachment of earnings if you do take them to court, so you really need to minimise debt as early as possible, as they don't earn anything if no rent is paid. But you should make sure you have a working or homeowner guarantor for every housing benefit property. In that case, you would chase the guarantor in much the same as you'd do with a working tenant.

If your tenant does not pay then that same day call them, and ask if they have paid or when you should go to pick up the rent. If you can't get through, go down that day and the next, keep knocking until you do get to speak to the tenant. Don't do this forcefully – just ask them when they will pay and if there is any reason why they have not done so.

Always try to get a standing order set up - fortnightly is often best, as that would keep it in line with their benefit payments. Try to get them to make the rent payment the day after they receive their benefit payment – this ensures the money is in their account but they won't have had time to spend it.

If you can't get through to the tenant within 72 hours, give the guarantor a call and say the rent has not been paid and can they contact the tenant to get payment. Also give them a 'heads up' that if payment is not made in the next three days it will be the guarantor making the payment. Having their mother, brother or good friend chasing them is often a stronger motivation than you calling them.

One thing to remember is housing benefit tenants differ in that you can have the LHA (Local Housing Allowance or what is commonly called housing benefit) paid directly to yourself from the start by having the right terms in your AST.

This works for most councils, but not all. Or if a tenant is in arrears, then under Part 12 regulation 95b of the housing benefit act 2006, if the tenant is eight weeks in arrears (not two months arrears, which is 8.67 weeks - this does make a difference) then the council must make direct payment to the landlord or agent.

If you have any queries about this or anything else, please contact us at questions@Property30.co.uk.

Students properties or HMOs are different again but if you have the property rented on one tenancy, then work in an equivalent way to housing benefit tenants. That is, act quickly, contact all the tenants and contact the guarantors as soon as possible.

If your property is rented on a room-by-room basis then you need to find out quickly if they are still in your property and what is happening with the rent. Call the tenant but if you are unable to contact them, ring another tenant in the property to find out if the non-paying tenant has been seen and when they are normally in.

If you still can't contact the tenant, go to the property at the time with the best chance of catching him or her in. If the tenant is working then the next stages will be similar to how I advised you to resolve any non-payment issues with working tenant. For the non-workers, you should, again, have a guarantor.

I will cover sections and court procedure tomorrow. Rest assured that rent arrears does not happen as often as you think or see on TV. I've only ever been to court once for a possession claim, even though I've dealt with hundreds of properties and thousands of tenants. If you get things done right at the beginning, and you're swift on rent collection, you should be able to stop any minor issues developing into full-blown crises.

25. Removing tenants

If you have got to the stage where you have to remove a tenant, either due to rent arrears or other issues, or if you just want the property vacant for you to move back into or to sell you need to issue a notice.

Remember, only a tenant or a judge can give your property back to you!

I'll say that again, only the tenant or a judge can give you the property back!

Now we've got that out of the way there are two types of section. If there's a blame there's a section eight - and a total of 17 grounds to cover everything from a temporary let, long-term let of a holiday lets to criminal activity. The main ground is ground eight - rent arrears of more than eight weeks if the rent is paid weekly, or two months if the rent is charged monthly. This is compulsory eviction if the terms are met.

The other type of notice is a Section 21. This is easily remembered as the 'no blame'. You just want to have the property back. This requires two months' notice but can be done without going to court through the accelerated possession procedure.

Serving a Section 21 used to be process-led in that if you did the right thing at the right time, you got your property back. However, since October 1st, 2015 this has all been changed. You must now ensure you supply a valid CP12 (gas check), issued a current EPC and supplied the tenant with the government manual 'How to rent' and protected the deposit and issued the tenant with the prescribed information. If any of this is not done, then no Section 21 eviction will be issued by the court.

In addition to this, if the tenant has repairs and you don't carry out the work and a council housing office issues you a notice, then you can't issue a Section 21 for six months. This was brought in to prevent retaliatory evictions by landlords.

I don't want you to be fearful of serving notice, but you will need to issue notice over time as a landlord. To focus a tenant on paying the rent by serving a Section 8 or if you want to refurb a property and serve a Section 21 have the form to hand, go through it and understand it.

I wanted to go through how to deal with tenants from the start, throughout and at the end because it is often not dealt with properly, and leaves many new investors confused over what they need to do.

There is a different legal system in Scotland and the tenancy laws have recently been changed. Please contact us at questions@Property30.co.uk for any advice.

26. Taking good photographs of your property

Taking photos of your property in the right way is the difference between having 30 people enquiring about your property or none. Now with the portals being so important for getting enquires, the one little photo in the long list of properties needs to stand out as it is the only thing that will make someone click to check out more about the property. Humans are visual beings and a property can be discounted in seconds if the photo is not right.

Try to get your photos on a sunny day, especially for the external pictures. Use a wide-angle lens or stand in the very corner of the rooms. Always look for things that are out of place - letters sticking out the of the letter box, the gate open, toys on the floor or clutter on the mantelpiece. For bathroom, have the towels neat and toilet seat down, no toothbrushes left cluttered on the sink or clothes hanging over the shower rail. in the kitchen, the sink and cooker need to be clean and tidy, with nothing on or in them.

For internals always have as much light in the room as possible - dark, dingy pictures do nothing to appeal to prospective buyers or tenants. Switch all ceiling and wall lights on, carry a tall lamp from room to room if it helps (just make sure it can't be seen in the pictures).

I would even go so far as to have professional pictures taken to show the property in the best light. You don't just need to go for the companies that specialise in this, but a semi-professional at a university or a local camera club will do so much better than you can and will have the equipment to produce the best photos.

As for equipment, an iPhone is not good enough for photos. They are OK for pictures of you and your friends for Facebook but it doesn't have the quality of picture for advertising property. Photos taken on smartphones just don't zing out of the screen (which you will see from the examples at Property30.co.uk).

A compact camera can do the job if you only have one or two properties but to get a wide-angle camera of sufficient quality will cost a few hundred pounds - maybe spending £50 per property to get photos taken professionally would be a better way to spend your money.

But if you do want to do it yourself, an SLR or Single Lens Reflex camera with interchangeable lens and a super wide-angle lens will set you back £300-£800, or even more if you want to get the very best. I would recommend a Canon 8 to 15mm costing upwards of £500 for the lens alone. This is not a cheap option and only for agents and big landlords (or a business expense for a new toy!).

I have uploaded to Property30.co.uk some photos of before and after, and some professional photos with a Canon 5d and a super wide angle and off camera flash - total cost over £2000 and that's not taking into account the post production and software needed.

I would suggest if you are going to be taking your own photos, rather than trying to learn how to get the photography right with time against you, test and improve your skills now. Practise taking photos of your own property see how you can get all your room in the picture, how light affects the image and what you missed when taking the photo that now screams out at you to take it again. Practice is the only thing that will help you, no matter what equipment you have at your disposal.

Give it a go and either email me at photo@Property30.co.uk or post on the Property30 Facebook group and I'll positively critique them to help you improve.

Go to Property30.co.uk see examples of good, bad and (maybe) ugly photos.

27. Systems

Systems are the evil masterpieces created by big business. They are contained in big manuals that never get read that are used by bosses to prevent your new idea or justify some command. Or that's how they are often thought of and it's ALL wrong!

Systems can be as simple as you want. They can be written on paper or on the computer, they can be audio or videos or screen recordings of what you do and when. They could be a checklist to ensure something is not missed or they could be having scissors on some string next to the filing cabinet to ensure you (or better still, someone else) has them at hand to cut documents before filing.

Your systems can be as difficult or as easy as you make them. They can be as long as you need them to be, but before worrying about how you will write them, worry about the person taking the information in.

Can they, without any prior knowledge or training, instruct anyone to do the task perfectly, every time. Now if you are thinking I work alone or you don't need this, then think again.

What if you expand and take on staff - do you want to issue all the instructions while doing the tasks and watching what they do? What if you are ill and stuck in bed or, worse still, in hospital unable to do any work? If you are out of the equation, does your business stop operating? What if you are on an extended break to fulfil one of your life's goals of travelling? Well, you won't be going anywhere if you try to do all of it by yourself.

So, I want you to look back at your time management exercise and examine what you spent most of your time on. Each and every task can be systemised and this will either prevent mistakes when you are doing the tasks, or reveal to you what can be given to a Virtual Assistant or staff member to make sure you are not the one doing the low-level tasks that take up time and don't contribute to your bottom line.

List your top five tasks from days 11 and then think of the best ways to systemise them. If you do credit checks, then record a video of your screen and show where you click and why, which options you choose etc. Don't put the password in there as it's a security risk and it will change over time. This video now becomes an evergreen training module. This is a done once, use again and again task.

Sit someone in front of a computer, click play and then they'll know what to do - simple. If it's your filing structure maybe have a sample property file pinned to the wall with an explanation of what should go into each plastic pocket. This ensures that if someone doesn't know or forgets how it goes (we all have those days) they can quickly refer to it. Then have a Monday morning check of three random files to ensure everything is going to plan.

So that is it for today. I have no template as I don't want to give you a template that restricts how or where you have your systems. Just make a start on it right away and build from there.

28. Systems Part 2

In this section, my good friend James Grew provides his input on the systems that he implements. I'm certain you will love how he describes how to make yourself redundant in your own business.

Systems and Automation – Making Yourself Redundant

So what exactly is a system? In my view, a system is a method of solving a repeated business issue in a strategic and effortless way.

One way of looking at it is as rules for your business: if this happens, then do this; but if that happens, then do that. These are codified, recorded and available to anyone. This takes all emotion out of decisions but also means that the same result is produced every time.

Why should you put systems in place in your business? Firstly, it will free up your time. Put simply, there is not enough time in the day to grow your business on your own.

If you are a one-man band and you want to double your revenue, then you have to double your hours. With systems in place you can get jobs done by other people, freeing up time for yourself to focus on the business rather than working in your business.

Secondly: legacy. If the worst was to happen, what would happen to your business? If your whole business is in your head, how will anyone know what to do? With systems, you are also building a truly valuable asset that is very saleable in the future.

A good system:

- Should address a specific problem within your business. Look at your processes and problems and then try and develop a solution for them. Creating a system for a problem that is not there will only add to your bureaucracy instead.

- Is documented. Anyone should be able to understand exactly how your system works, no matter what their learning style. All of my manuals include both a video and a text document, with a checklist of the process at the end to ensure nothing is missed.

- Has an owner. Who is ultimately responsible for this section? People should feel ownership for their particular tasks to encourage productivity, but this also gives a starting point of who to ask if it has not been done.

- Is scalable. When you put a system in place, you want it to work if you are selling one widget or if you are selling 100. There is no point in developing a system that you have to change later on.

- Is measurable. You want a system that you can easily measure, not just for you but also for your staff so they can assess their progress. This is where KRA (Key Result Areas) come into play.

- Is automated. There are a lot of things out there that can be automated, relieving you and your employees of extra tasks, thus saving you time and money.

- Is consistent. It will produce the same result every time. The system needs to be easy to use for everyone so that everyone understands.

I have some specific rules that I use in my property management systems:

- Only input data once. I want the data to flow from one piece of software to the next rather than type the same data into every piece of software I use.

- Never type numbers. It is very easy to type £9.98 instead of £9.99 and it can throw your calculations out.

- Create rules. I would rather spend five minutes creating a rule or system than having to do a one-minute job multiple times. I am always looking for long-term gain rather than short-term reward.

My entire system revolves around Xero. Xero (www.xero.co.uk) is a cloud-based accountancy package. It works using a direct link to your bank account or credit card to automatically import every transaction made into the software.

Your job is then to tell Xero what each transaction is, for example rent or mortgage. Xero then files the transactions in a folder so you can retrieve them again when you are doing your tax return or just looking at your profit and loss statement.

Receipt Bank (www.receipt-bank.com) is an app that takes a lot of the pain out of book-keeping. After inputting your receipt or invoices to Receipt Bank, by scanning, taking a picture or emailing it directly, it will then process the receipt and automatically import the details of the supplier, date, invoice number, tax amount and overall total.

This data is then filed and saved in the cloud. Once the files have been processed, this data can then be sent to be reconciled against a payment on your bank account within Xero. For example, if you were to buy a new office chair on Amazon, Amazon will email you a receipt.

You can forward this on to Receipt Bank, which processes the invoice and works out exactly what it is and the total amount and tax. You can then tell Receipt Bank this needs to be filed in the 'Office Furniture' folder.

Following this, you send this information to Xero, and can then find the payment that was made to Amazon and match it with the receipt that has been imported from Receipt Bank and reconcile it.

All I have done is forward the receipt, select the correct folder and confirmed the transaction in Xero. I have not typed in any data and I have only put the data in once and it has flowed between the two pieces of software automatically.

Arthur Property Management (www.arthuronline.co.uk) works as my property CRM (customer relationship management) package. It is a very powerful bit of software. As a property manager, you have overall access, but can then give landlords access to see their rent statements and also which properties are full etc.

Your tenants can also gain access to see their rent statements and report any issues to you directly. You can also send work orders to your contractors with the tenants' details so they can contact them directly without you being the middle man.

Within Arthur you can keep a track of outstanding tasks, rents due, and empty properties. You can also keep a track of all of your tenancies and have all of your tenancy information and contact details in one place.

The main advantage of Arthur, however, is the link to Xero. When a tenant pays your rent into the bank, you can reconcile it automatically and pay it off in their rent book within Arthur. This means that you keep a very close track of any rent outstanding or due from your tenants.

The power is not in these apps themselves, even though on their own they are also very powerful, but in how they link together, and how the data flows from one app to the next. This is where a powerful system is created.

I also now record myself doing any task that I set within these programmes using a screen-capture software called Jing (www.techsmith.com/jing-tool.html). I send this recording to my virtual assistant who creates a manual for exactly how the job is done.

This is then filed. I can then get one of my virtual assistants to do the job next time. If they cannot do it, I can refer them back to the manual describing how the task was made before.

I am taking me out of the business, not just so I can focus on other things but also so that if the worst were to happen, people would know what to do without me.

I help people in a wide variety of businesses put great systems together. I love doing this and my main aim is to make every small business in the country more productive and do the things that they really enjoy doing, without having to spend hours doing unnecessary data entries.

If you would like any more help please feel free to contact me on james@systems2success.co.uk or on my website www.systems2success.co.uk

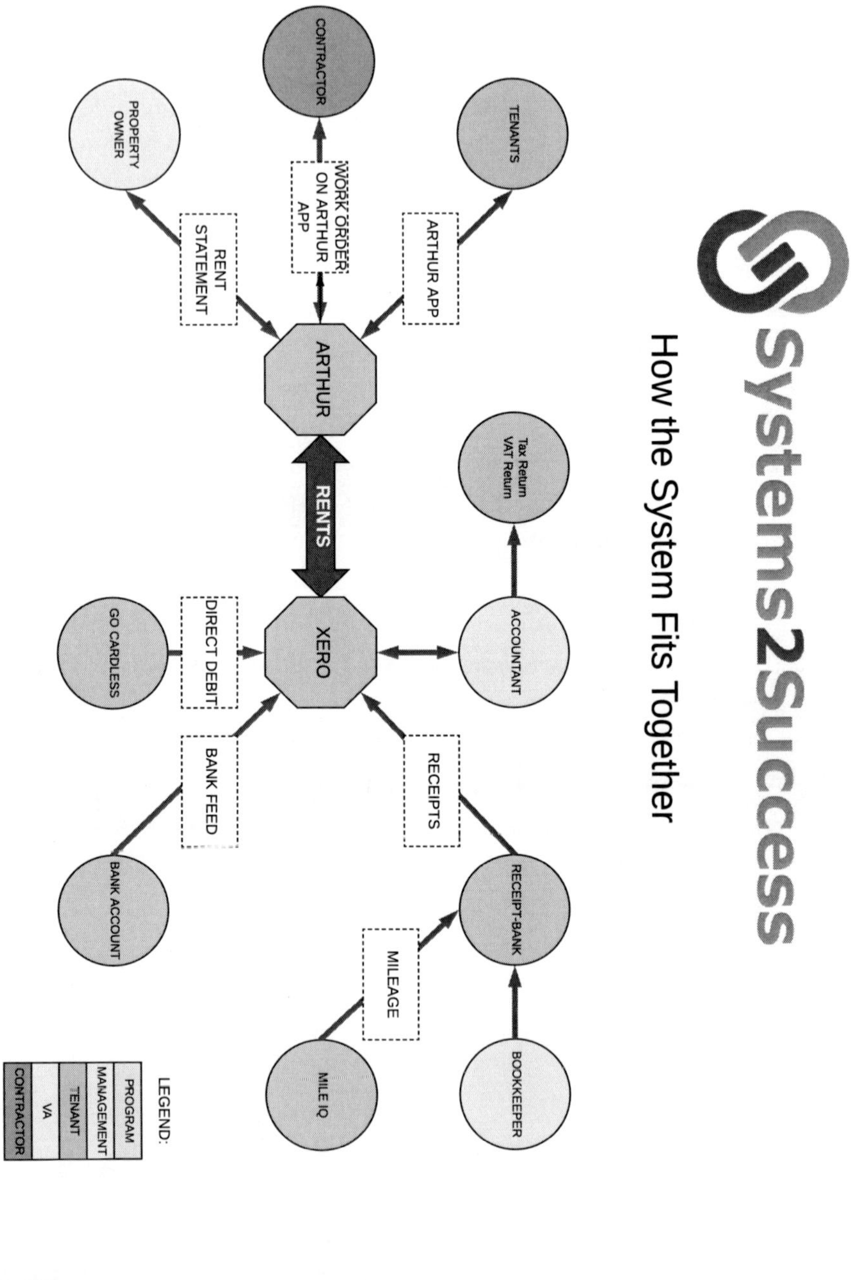

Systems2Success
How the System Fits Together
CONTRACTOR
PROPERTY OWNER
TENANTS
WORK ORDER ON ARTHUR APP
RENT STATEMENT
ARTHUR APP
ARTHUR
RENTS
XERO
Tax Return
VAT Return
ACCOUNTANT
GO CARDLESS
DIRECT DEBIT
BANK FEED
RECEIPTS
BANK ACCOUNT
RECEIPT-BANK
MILEAGE
BOOKKEEPER
MILE IQ
LEGEND:
PROGRAM
MANAGEMENT
TENANT
VA
CONTRACTOR

29. Reviewing your goals: from day eight

Today is the penultimate day and I wanted to review your goals from day eight - you did write them down, I hope? Now I want you to get them out or find where they are pinned to the wall and really reflect on what you set as your goals.

Do they still reflect what you now want? Do they give you the challenge and incentive to push through the obstacles, that will stand in the way, for you to succeed, or have your goals changed or already been completed?

Should you make your goals bigger or should you change them altogether?

You need to look at your goals frequently, at least weekly and preferably daily, as it gives you a reminder of what you want to achieve. This will give you a kick up the bum to get on with your plans and keep you on track so you do not waver from these goals on shiny new things that get offered to you by people you come into contact with.

I have attached a sample goal, which you are free to use, or alternatively use your own list. I have my goals entered into Evernote and renew them every six months - annually is too long. But I keep the old list of goals so I can compare what my challenges were then and see how far I have come. I then have my iPhone as a background image to remind me of my goals every time I look at my phone. Get the sample at Property30.co.uk.

30. Congratulations

I thought it was important to celebrate the fact that, no matter where you started 30 days ago that you have moved forward in your property business (or maybe you just picked this book up in the bookshop – if that is the case, then go to the front and read from the beginning you cheater!)

This full-month training can help you achieve the level of freedom that you want, be that a side income to park your money, for replacing your current income or for immense wealth and the trappings that it affords.

You and you alone hold the information in this book and the power to use it to move you forward.

Now I know it is not always easy to get the time to read this book and put the tasks within each task into practice. Hopefully you have been reading and listening to the daily chapters, going through the exercises and using the accompanying website Property30.co.uk, and I'm sure you can see now how worthwhile it has all been.

But I also want to remind you that this is a journey and, as such, you should enjoy the journey as much as the rewards. It is so important to stop and appreciate where you are now and how far you have come. Be sure to reward yourself at milestones along that journey to success.

It is no good waiting for the big day where you own the specified number of properties or have a large monthly income, as I very much see that as a mystical day - like trying to find the end of the rainbow. Instead, as your grow bigger your goals grow bigger still, so you will always have more to do and more to achieve. Ultimately, you'll never be totally happy just chasing the money alone.

Always remember why you are doing this. I'm sure it's not just for the sake of success alone, but to have the lifestyle and freedom for yourself and your family that probably only property is going to give you.

This is a gift to you, an invitation if you will, to return, as and when you need, as this is a journey and not a destination.

Here's to your property success.

BONUS CHAPTER

Now for something a bit different. Assuming you've just read the whole book (and not cheated by skipping right to the end!) you'll be ready to get cracking on your life-changing and life-affirming mission to create financial security for you and your loved ones over the next month. But, as we've stated, it's important to keep yourself in the right frame of mind, especially when the going gets a little bit tough. I've always been very inspired by people who have manufactured their own destinies and I'm 100 per cent convinced that running your own life - your way - is the surest route to contentment It doesn't matter where you are right now (and I've probably been in lower places), it's where you're going to be when you take full control. Please allow me to entertain and hopefully enlighten you with the following reference from literature and cinema of how one troubled man was able to turn dirt into gold-dust.

The late German/American author Charles Bukowski is rarely held up as a positive example to follow for budding entrepreneurs and businessmen.

Bukowski wrote from his own bitter experience about life on the edge of minimum-wage poverty in Los Angeles from the Great Depression of the 1930s until people started buying his books in the late 1950s, and he became a minor celebrity of his time.

From pretty much the onset of his adolescence, Bukowski was a confirmed alcoholic and his semi-autobiographical short stories and poems chronicled what it was like to be caught in the poverty trap where even regular pay checks couldn't alleviate the pain of being stuck in a downward vortex.

That probably chimes with most people today, caught in the rat trap of living from pay check to pay check and only one life-changing event, such as redundancy or a bad health scare, away from seeing your world and everything you have worked for crumbling around your shoulders.

Bukowski, like others of his generation, stood for the outlaw, the outsider. In an era where most people in the 'rich countries' had regular, steady work and on the surface seemed to live comfortable lives, whether they were working class or middle class, he saw through the lie.

The following is a quote from him (slightly truncated for reasons of good taste) which still chimes with me about 20 years after I first read it, and was one of the major reasons why I give up comfortable full-time employment nearly 10 years ago to live a life of more freedom and opportunity.

Bukowski: "How in the hell could a man enjoy being awakened at 6:30am by an alarm clock, leap out of bed, dress, force-feed, brush teeth and hair, and then fight traffic to get to a place where essentially you made lots of money for somebody else and were asked to be grateful for the opportunity to do so?"

I'm sure most readers can relate to this at some level, and if you can't, you are probably reading the wrong book and I'd suggest your precious time would be better spent updating your CV and browsing the online jobs listings.

If you're still with me, you are feeling some pain, some lack, in your life that is propelling you towards a future that can be as bright as you want it to be.

There is obviously such a thing as a rich and successful employee, and if that's your perceived destiny, I sincerely wish you the very best of luck.

But when you're fully aware that your destiny is in the hands of someone else, it's inevitable that this lack of control will lead to self-doubt, depression and a loss of identity. These are some of the major psychological problems of our time and it's only going to get worse.

You're either designing your own life or it's being designed for you by someone else, and almost entirely for their benefit, not yours.

Although the era of the 9-5, job for life, gold watch and hit the golf course until you die may have gone, the same principles apply, only the deal is even more rotten now than it used to be.

School leavers and university graduates alike are finding it increasingly difficult to gain meaningful, purposeful and properly remunerated employment. You will relate to this if you are in your late teens/early 20s or have relatives in an age range where people should be having the best times of their lives.

It's said that this is the first generation since the dawn of the industrial revolution (roughly the late 18th century until the mid-19th century) to earn less and have a lower quality of life than their parents.

This is a tragic set of affairs for those caught in the 21st century poverty trap, where it's estimated a school leaver today (2018) can expect to work until the age of 69 with nothing like the same pension benefits, public or private.

Metaphorically speaking, the treadmill of mediocrity that applies to most wage slaves in the modern economy has now gone into reverse. Not only are the upcoming generation expected to work harder and longer in brain-numbingly banal jobs, but they'll have less to show for it at the end of their productive lives. They'll go from wage poverty to actual poverty and nobody has a clue what to do about it.

And what is it all for anyway? Let's take the five days on, two days off model as the standard norm for a working week, even though more and more people are expected to conform to health-destroying shift patterns and the infamous 'Zero hour' contracts (similar to itinerant labourers in Third World Countries sitting at the side of a dusty road at 5am hoping to get asked to jump in the back of a pick-up truck to go and earn a few pennies).

So, all other things remaining equal, the traditional worker is investing five days of their time to earn two days of freedom, where they can devote their hours to the things that matter to them like family, hobbies, self-development etc.

It's not exactly a great return or investment or a fulfilling way to live your life: handing over five days of your life to a faceless company or public body in exchange for 48 hours when you can do what you like.

And as most of us can appreciate, you'll spend the latter half of your Sunday thinking about going back to work on the Monday morning, so you can never really escape the treadmill of work, whether physically or psychologically.

This is exactly why the school week runs on a five days on, two days off basis. It's not because it's the most effective way to educate children to the best of their abilities, it's main function is to prepare children for the realities of an 'ordinary' working life.

This is also why the concept of the 'weekend' is so sanctified in western, and some other cultures. Think of all the songs, films, plays etc. that glorify those precious two days 'off' at the end of five days selling your labour for someone else's benefit. How much can you cram in? How drunk can you get?

It's no different to imagine that the reason why hundreds of thousands of people, especially in the 18-45 demographic, get hammered every Friday and Saturday is because they want to erase the memories of the previous five days and try not to think about the upcoming work week. In essence, it's a psychic defence against reality.

Is that a healthy way to live your life? I'll leave you to decide. And we haven't even considered the release of the pressure valve that constitutes what is today called annual leave.

This is why so many people are so angry and depressed about life and employment today. Even though working conditions were much harsher for our ancestors, even when you just go back a couple of generations, the average modern worker is educated and savvy enough to know that he's getting a poor deal. And the frustrating thing is that he doesn't know how to get out of it. In essence, he feels trapped.

From the start of written history until the dawn of the 20th century, every man and woman knew their place in a strict and rigid societal structure.

If you were born a peasant, you died a peasant. The concept of promotion and 'getting on' in life was totally unknown, so you just got on with it and hoped you wouldn't get wiped out in one of your king's wars or contracted a terrible disease like Bubonic Plague.

However, in today's world we have 24/7 exposure to the lifestyles of the rich and famous and we assume we can never get access to the existence of our dreams as we flick through celebrity magazines during our 10-minute coffee breaks.

We know the good life is out there somewhere and we assume we can never get over that rainbow but the good news is that we can. The shocking news is that you'll never get there if you opt to stay in full-time employment. There's your reality check, right there.

The most effective way to get on in life, and it's fully time-tested, is to get yourself educated, start your own business (you can be a sole trader or run a limited company, among other options) and make a success of that business.

There's nothing more satisfying in the world of work than being your own boss and creating wealth for yourself, your family, your community and beyond. And then leaving a legacy.

If you've read this far in the book, congratulations. You have proved you're dedicated to improving your life and finally breaking free. If we can help you in any way, please get in touch using any of the following methods and we'll be happy to point you in the right direction.

Paul Baldry: 01670 800 029

Andy McInnes: 07795 086526

Facebook: Property30